SALZBURG
LUTHERAN
EXPULSION
AND
ITS IMPACT

Samuel Urlsperger, Pastor of St. Anne's, Augsburg

Salzburg Lutheran

Expulsion

and Its Impact

CARL MAUELSHAGEN

*Professor Emeritus of History, Georgia State College,
Atlanta, Georgia*

VANTAGE PRESS

NEW YORK   WASHINGTON   HOLLYWOOD

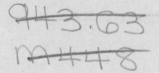
FIRST EDITION

Copyright, 1962, by Carl Mauelshagen

Published by Vantage Press, Inc.
120 West 31st Street, New York 1, N.Y.

Manufactured in the United States of America

TO

MY WIFE

ADELE MAUELSHAGEN

PREFACE

MY INTEREST in the Salzburgers of Germany was aroused by the stories which I heard about them and about their descendants soon after 1935, when I assumed my duties as Professor of History at what is now Georgia State College in Atlanta. A casual reading of fragmentary accounts about the trek of the Salzburgers to Georgia between 1733 and 1740 convinced me that an investigation of the reasons for their expulsion from Salzburg would be a profitable study. This became more obvious when I searched through the sources on the Georgia Salzburgers in the De'Renn Collection of the University of Georgia at Athens.

To my amazement the University of Chicago libraries had a wealth of source material upon the expulsion of the Protestants by Prince-Archbishop Firmian between 1731 and 1734. Here were accessible many thousands of pages of contemporary material for anyone with the patience and perseverance to wade through these German sources. In these, Firmian was extolled by some and condemned by others for expelling about one seventh of the total population of his principality. As the refugees trudged into northern Europe they were reviled by a few but as soon as they reached the Protestant areas of Europe they were extolled, wined, dined and likened to the children of Israel who fled from Egypt into the land of promise.

This work was expanded into a short history of Salzburg when I found no such study in the English and only two in the German language. One of these, now a rare book, was published in 1873, the other, a voluminous work of three volumes and approximately 1300 pages, was published in 1907. There is no reference of a a history of Salzburg to be found in the catalogue of the Library of Congress. If a history on Salzburg were at all available, I most certainly would have found it for sale and on display in its book shops. Such a work would be purchased by many of the thousands of English-speaking tourists who annually are attracted to this quaint as well as modern city by its scenic grandure and its world famous Music Festival.

Located between Germany and Austria, Salzburg was inevitably drawn into the currents of European history. Its extensive salt deposits in the *Salzkammergut* and in the *Duerrnberg* at Hallein, its outcroppings of high grade iron ore and gold made Salzburg a pawn in the game of Germany diplomacy. The city of Salzburg, on the Lug pass athwart the Salza River, holds a commanding position on the main route of travel between the Danubian plateau and northern Italy. This line of communication is crossed by a less important one from the east. In the past, Roman Legions, early Christian missionaries, barbarian Germans and Huns and armies of contending European powers marched along these trade routes.

I am deeply indebted to my colleagues Professors Hal Hulsey, James E. Routh and Gaines W. Walter, who have read all of the manuscript and offered many helpful suggestions. Dr. Gaines W. Walter's critical analysis of the basic historical facts was especially helpful to me. While I thankfully acknowledge their services, which contributed toward this work, it is only fair to relieve them of any errors which may have crept into this study.

The Reverend Dr. Lindenmeyer, Deacon and pastor of St. Anne's Church in Augsburg, Germany, his staff and Dr. Frederick Blendinger, the archivist of the city of Augsburg, gave generously of their time to orient me on the political and religious affairs of the city when the refugees from Salzburg converged on it. Through the courtesy of the pastor of St. Anne's, I was able to obtain several copies of paintings of Salzburgers en route through Augsburg. The management of the Parkhotel Kaiserhof of Salzburg, where I resided when in Salzburg, graciously permitted me to have two rare pictures at the Kaiserhof photographed to be used for this book. My wife and I could not have seen the city and the former prince-archbishopric as advantageously as we did had it not been for the management of the Kaiserhof Hotel.

In conclusion, I wish to express my appreciation for the interest and the cooperation of the librarians and archivists of the following institutions for making available to me the sources for this book: the University of Chicago, Georgia State College and Emory University in Atlanta, The University of Georgia, Athens, the University at Salzburg, the University of Munich, Germany and the University of Vienna, Austria, the state archives of Bavaria, Munich, and of Austria, Vienna and the city archives of Augsburg.

CONTENTS

Survey in Salzburg—Military Precautions Taken by
Firmian—Imperial Forces Sent to Salzburg—Arrest of
Protestant Leaders—Protestants Disarmed—Provocative
Acts of Firmian

Catholic-Protestant Cleavage—Ominous Days Ahead—
Expulsion Procedure—Confusion Due to Lack of Plan-
ning—Contagion of Forced March—Property Holders
Refused to Be Persuaded—Emigration Dues Assessed—
Last March into Uplands—Exodus Across Frontier
Stalled—Berchtesgaden Lutherans Ask Permission to
Leave

Dilemma of Emperor Charles VI—The Terms of West-
phalia vs. Firmian's Policy—Refugees Tricked into
Assuming Responsibility—Firmian and Emperor at
Linz—Lutherans and Calvinists Unite for Relief—
Threat of Protestant Princes—Firmian Makes Best of
International Issue—King of Prussia Offers a Haven to
the Refugees—Europe Opens Hearts and Purses

Enthusiastic Reception of Emigrants—Tales of Miracles—
Catholic Sympathy—Evidence of Opposition to Mass
Movement into Prussia—Augsburg, a Lutheran Shrine
and Place of Refuge—Commemorative Coins

Samuel Urlsperger As a Benevolent Promoter—Misgiv-
ings and Assurances—First Transport for America—
Emigrants Extolled—Preparations for Settlement at Ebenezer—Next Three Transports for Georgia

Trends in Salzburg Since 1731—Firmian's Anti-Lutheran
Zeal Remains Unabated—End of Systematic Persecution—Change in Religious Policy in Salzburg Fails to Halt

SALZBURG
LUTHERAN
EXPULSION
AND
ITS IMPACT

CHAPTER I

GEOGRAPHY, NATURAL RESOURCES, AND PEOPLE OF SALZBURG

IT WOULD be difficult to find in all of Europe another area of about 330-350 square miles which abounds in scenic beauty and panoramic grandeur as does the bishopric of Salzburg. Few prelates of Europe from the ninth to the nineteenth century could match the bishop of Salzburg in spiritual and temporal prestige. Its geographical position enabled its ruler and his country to escape some of the more tragic events in European history. On occasions the archbishop was able to make the best of his key geographical position to obtain valuable concessions from German emperors and to safeguard the security of his principality by siding first with one and then with another of his more powerful neighbors.

Perhaps for the sake of brevity the ancient Latin name of Salzburg, *Civitas Clavdia*[1] was called Juvavum. As yet scholars are not fully agreed upon the exact meaning of the Roman names. Seventeenth century scholars thought Juvavum meant "helfen" (help) and therefore called it "Helfenburg", a place where Roman reserves were stationed in readiness to re-enforce the imperial army in case of a breach along the Danube of the Rhine-Danube defense line of the Roman army against the barbarian Germans. In the eighteenth century the derivative of Juvavum was thought to be *juva,* from *juvare,* meaning aid or help, and *via,* meaning way; since the city guarded the way from Italy to the Danube through the Roman province of Noricum along the middle Danube.

---

[1]*Encyclopedia Britannica,* 14th edition, 1915 (Unsigned article). "The site has been occupied since pre-Roman time, the original settlement being replaced by a Roman trading town Juvavum sacked by the barbarians (477)."

15

At the time of Julius Caesar (59-44 B.C.) Roman detachments had been quartered at "Helfenburg" as re-enforcements for the army along the Danube. During the age of German migration the area of Noricum belonged first to one and then to another of the barbarian tribes. It was in the fifth century that German military leaders in the Roman army succeeded in making and unmaking Roman emperors at will. The last of these, called Romulus Augustulus, "the Little Augustus," was quietly displaced by the German soldiers who put one of their number, Odoacer, in his place (476). It is believed that Attila, the leader of the Huns, on his thrust into western Europe in the first half of the fifth century put the city to the torch. About a quarter century later (around 477) Odoacer completed the destruction of Juvavum, which lay waste for more than a century, when it passed under the jurisdiction of the Duke of Bavaria. Salzburg as known today was founded around 700 A.D. by Rupert, an itinerant missionary, and in time became the seat of a bishop, and of an archbishop, and later on an independent principality.

Much of the province of Salzburg is a geographical unit drained by the Salzach formed by numerous Alpine streams. In the Moravian plateau of Bavaria the crystal clear water of the Salzach pours into the Inn, a tributary of the Danube. This triangular shaped principality "is a country of dark blue lakes hemmed in by green meadows and woods, of steep mountain slopes and precipitous peaks."[2] Its apex points northward, and its base nestles in the Tyrolese Alps. To the east it is bounded by the provinces of upper Austria, Styria, Carinthia and the Tyrol, and on the west by Bavaria. Set in it almost as an enclave, with but a narrow opening into Bavaria, is Berchtesgaden, a medieval seat of a monastic principality called the "Rupertiwinkel," a gift to Rupertus "bishop" and patron saint of Salzburg. From the hills of the town of Salzburg one obtains a panoramic view of the town bisected by the Salzach and of the picturesque valleys flanked to the east by the peaks of Mount Hohenstaufen, today called the Watzmann. This wonderland of nature is traversed by the most important north-south line of communication between the Danubian plateau and Italy. A less

---

[2]*Illustrated Guide-book through Salzburg-Town and its Environs,* (Oestereichisches Propogandabuero Salzburg).

16

important passage from the east to the Alpine Tyrol in the west intercepts the north-south road near the town of Salzburg. Ranging in altitudes of thousands of feet, some of the majestic mountains are capped in perpetual snow. Fed by the melting snow, the mountain streams, as they cascade down the precipitous mountain crags, are wrapped in mist, and are white with foam in their plunge toward the Salzach. The latter follows an easterly course through a narrow valley, the Pinzgau, between the Tauern and the Salzburg Alps. At the approximate focal point of the Salzburg triangle, the Salzach turns abruptly toward the north. In its northward course at *Wildshut,* the seat of an old hunting castle, the river leaves the triangle at its apex. The principality of Salzburg is divided into five districts, *Gaue,* the Flachgau which includes the capital city and the Salzkammergut, the Tennengau with the salt-mining town of Hallein and the *Duerrnberg,* a mountain from which salt has been extracted since primitive times. The mountain sides of Salzburg overlook picturesque valleys studded with peasant holdings. The white homes with red tile roofs, set in shaded lawns and wooded groves, form a restful setting in the scenic Alpine landscape.

The only city in the province is Salzburg, the birthplace of Wolfgang Mozart. It has an elevation of 1430 feet and lays claim to a population today which has grown from 40,000 in 1938 to over 110,000. Its two tallest mountains, the *Moenchsberg* and the *Kapuzienerberg*, with its Capuchin monastery, guard the important pass, the *Lug,* which was cut through the mountains by the river Salza at Salzburg. The pass at this point is scarcely wide enough to accommodate the flow of traffic along the main road which extends from the Danubian plateau in the north to Italy in the south. Atop the Moenchsberg is the fortress *Hohensalzburg,* the largest and best preserved fortress of central Europe. At the Lug a less important east-west road intersects the one from the north to the south.

Extending from the crescent shaped valley, formed by the Salzach at Salzburg, are finger like valleys made by Alpine rivulets. These are carpeted with a lush growth of grass and succulent herbs which afford an abundant pasturage from early spring until later summer. As soon as the tender blades of grass project themselves above the melting snow, herdsmen and maids start the gradual drive of cattle through the verdant valleys into the uplands. Here

17

they remain until the late summer, when they return with quantities of cheese made from flavorful milk and with their herds of fattened cattle for the markets of Bavaria and Austria. However, the income from the sale of these articles and that obtained from the sale of grain must be augmented through other occupations to maintain the economy of this frugal mountain folk.

Since primitive times salt in considerable quantities has been obtained in the principality of Salzburg. Artifacts found in the salt mines of the *Duerrnberg* (withered or dry mountain) at Hallein, the second largest and most important industrial town of the province, attest to this fact. Today a thriving chemical industry has evolved at the foot of the mountain where the water is evaporated from the brine extracted in the salt mine. The prevalence of salt accounts for such names as that of the province and the capital city Salzburg and its chief river, the Salzach. Outcroppings of copper, silver and gold were not uncommon. Centuries before the industrial revolution, small iron-working communities sprang up in places where ore outcroppings of high metallic content were discovered. The Greek historian Polybius (second century B.C.) tells of the discovery of rich deposits of gold along the upper source of the Drau and the Mur in Salzburg. When the Latins heard of this they rushed in and, with the aid of the natives, exploited this resource until driven out by the Etruscans. The subsequent "gold war," in which the treasure-trove was taken first by one and then the other, did not end until the Latins in the first century before Christ made themselves masters of this territory.

The rich gold deposits, discovered at the very time when the Spanish conquistadors were exploiting the rich deposits of the precious metals in the New World, were to a degree responsible for the inflationary spiral of the sixteenth and seventeenth centuries in Europe. Like the kings, the spiritual as well as the temporal princes of Europe found it necessary to obtain new sources of income to meet rising prices and to maintain an extravagant court. The prince bishop of Salzburg was therefore obliged to turn to the salt mines, the marble quarries, the iron mines, and the widely scattered gypsum mines for additional revenue.[3]

---

[3]Widman, Hans, *Geschichte Salzburgs*, V. I, pp. 9, 10, 286, 287; II, pp. 33, 174, (Gotha 1914).

Archaeologists have found considerable evidence of the presence of Neolithic and Bronze age man in the Salzburg region. Artifacts, such as flint arrowheads, splinters of pottery with thin line and hand decorations, grinding stones and hammers made of serpentine, usually green in color with spots resembling a serpent, have been found. Articles showing man's transition from the Neolithic, late stone age, to the Bronze age are not uncommon. Beyond this, little is known of the primitive inhabitants. They were either conquered, absorbed, or wiped out by the Keltic invaders from the West when they penetrated deeply into the Alpine country in the fourth century before Christ.

Generally speaking, the Salzburgers of today are of Austro-Bavarian stock. Their dialect is much like that of the eastern Bavarians, varying in accent from the softer variety spoken in the lowlands to the harsher type in highland Germany. Their climactic and highland environment has tended to make them a healthy, robust, industrious, and fairly tall folk who are loyally bound to their homeland, and who are likewise cheerful, honest, hospitable, and freedom loving. They live in communities scattered along lines of communications, in fertile valleys, near mineral spring resorts and mining regions.

CHAPTER II

FROM CHRISTIAN COMMUNITY TO BISHOPRIC (FROM ANTIQUITY TO 740 A. D.)

GEOGRAPHY, more than any factor, thrust Salzburg into the currents of European history. Adolph Buehler[1] quite aptly describes Salzburg's place in history in his *Salzburg seine Monumente und seine Fuersten*:

> Practically every foot of ground in this famed city conjures up memories from the past. Every stone seems to have a story to tell which is intimately associated not only with German but with Occidental history. Were they able to speak they might tell of the greatness of the Roman Empire, its decline and its fusion with the more vigorous Christian-Germanic civilization. Here it was that the early missionaries sowed the seed of Christianity. The city of Salzburg found itself enveloped in the tragic and demoralizing conflict between the papacy and the empire. This poisonous struggle steeped in lie, deceit, perjury, blasphemy, and immorality gnawed away at the vitals of human decency. At the close of the twelfth century, when the conflict between the imperialists and anti-imperialists had reached a crisis, Salzburg emerged as a modern state. The remark of the last of its prince-bishops, "make the best of your opportunity," was all too often the policy of many of his predecessors.

Christianity found its way into the Roman province of Noricum by way of the ancient trade routes extending northward from Rome and westward from the Syrian coast of Asia Minor into Noricum. Missionaries from Constantinople, Antioch, and other cities along the eastern Mediterranean, traveling over the old Syrian

---

[1]Buehler, Adolph, *Salzburg seine Monumente und seine Fuersten*, (Salzburg, 1873), pp. 1-20.

trade route and from Rome, followed a northerly course through the Alps, thence along the course of the Salzach and the Inn rivers to the Danube. In time, Christian communities of considerable size were to be found in places like Salzburg and *Regensburg* (Ratisbon) on the Danube. From the *Kreuzkapelle* (Chapel of the Holy Cross 1170) hard by the *Peterskirchhof* (St. Peter's Cemetery) in Salzburg a staircase, carved out of the rock of the Moenchsberg, leads to the catacombs. They are the only catacombs of early Christian times in central Europe still preserved in such good condition. Through *Gertrudenkapelle* (St. Gertrude's chapel) in the catacombs one reaches the *Kapelle des Hl. Maximus* (St. Maxim's Chapel).[2] Here this saint is said to have suffered the death of a martyr by being hurled down the side of the rocky cliff. St. Severus relates that in the fifth century, at the time of the Germanic migrations, there was hardly a hamlet westward from Salzburg to the Chiemsee, a lake about thirty miles west of Salzburg, and northward to the Danube, without a Christian Church having altars graced by gold or silver ceremonial vessels.

These outlying Christian communities were only slightly, if at all, affected by the Roman persecutions. Located as they were along these crossroads, they could hardly be expected to escape the impact of the doctrinal conflicts which split the Christian communities into hostile factions. The most serious of these was the clash between Athanasius and Arius, respectively archbishop and priest of Alexandria in Egypt. The latter taught that God is from eternity but that the Son and the Holy Spirit are his creation. This was a serious challenge to the Trinitarian doctrine advocated by Athanasius. He and most of the churchmen of the West held to the doctrine of a Godhead of three persons co-equal and co-eternal.

Emperor Constantine (324-337 A. D.) could hardly ignore such a threat to unity within the Roman Empire at a time when its European borders were menaced by the German babarians. For security and administrative purposes he had transferred the seat of government from Rome to the site of the ancient Greek town of Byzantium on the European side of the Bosporus and named it Constantinople. To put an end to the religious schism, he ordered the Christian prelates of the empire to meet at Nicæa in 325. This

---

[2]*Illustrated Guide-Book through Salzburg-Town and its Environs,* pp. 17, 18.

ecummenical council, presided over by Constantine, was the first of its kind in Christian history.

After heated debate, the Nicaean Creed was adopted. It upheld Trinitarianism as the orthodox doctrine and condemned Arianism as a heresy. In spite of this Arianism persisted in the eastern part of the empire and in areas like Salzburg along the eastern road of communication. For more than a century and a half the threat to orthodoxy was heightened by the Arian Germanic tribes east of the Danube and north of the Black Sea. They had been converted to the Arian faith and afterwards they penetrated into the heartland of the Roman world. By 481 they had set up Arian states in Gaul, Spain, Africa, and Italy.

Had it not been for the German Franks along the eastern bank of the lower Rhine, their kings, their alliance with the Roman papacy and their subsequent imperial policy, Arianism might well have triumphed in Europe. The conversion of Clovis, King of the Franks (481-511), and his warriors to the orthodox faith at the time of their conquest of Gaul made for a bond of fellowship between the conqueror and the conquered. The alliance with the Roman See was advantageous to both. For from that time on the Pope could look to the king of the Franks to come to his aid against the Arian Lombard king of Italy. On the other hand, the king of the Franks had every reason to expect a papal blessing for his ambitious program of incorporating willy-nilly all of the Germanic tribes of Europe into an orthodox Frankish empire in which the Pope would be recognized as the spiritual head.

A similar tribal expansion of pagan Germans along the eastern Slavic frontier took place almost simultaneously. In fact, years before the ambitious plan of the Franks had reached the border land of the Saxons, Bavarians, Franconians, and Alamanni, these so-called stem duchies[3] were well on the way toward political and cultural unity.

By the sixth century the duke of Bavaria, who had annexed the Roman province of Noricum, had recognized the nominal overlordship of the king of the Franks. However, degeneracy of the royal family, court intrigue, and attacks along the frontier of the kindom of the Franks enabled the Bavarian duke to ignore his over-

---

[3]Derived from the German, Stamm. Stem or hereditary duchies.

lord. For almost two centuries the independence of Bavaria was virtually unchallenged.

Not until the chief officer of the royal household, the Mayor of the Palace, had stabilized affairs of the realm by assuming regal authority was the independence of Bavaria challenged. Years before, Charles Martel (714-741), Mayor of the Palace, and his father took direct military action against Bavaria, they encouraged a policy of Frankish cultural infiltration into Bavaria. To this end the close bond of Pepin II, Martel's son, and Pope Zacharias proved of mutual advantage. When the pope was hard pressed by the Arian Lombards of Italy in 751 and badly needed Pepin's aid, the Mayor asked Zacharias to rule on his status in the empire of the Franks. The Roman See responded: "It seems better that he who has the power in the state should be called king than he who is falsely called king." Soon thereafter Boniface, missionary to the Germans and papal legate, anointed Pepin king of the Franks and threatened his subjects with excommunication should they choose a king from any other family. By virtue of this act, Pepin, the first of the Carolingian kings, became God's anointed in the sight of the church.

One of the first such emissaries sent from the West to propagandize for the Franks in Bavaria was Emmeram. From 660 to 670, as an itinerant bishop affiliated with the Gaelic church of Ireland, he laid the foundation for a bishopric in Regensburg, Bavaria. In a similar capacity Rupert (Herodbert, 696 to 718), probably a descendant of a ducal family of the district of Worms, set out with the blessing of the Mayor of the Palace in search of a place from which to work toward the propagation of the orthodox faith and the organization of Christian communities. On his journey down the Danubian plain he reached Rassau in Bavaria, a place where the Inn empties into the Danube, and from there he followed its course to its confluence with the Salzach. Following up the course of the latter to the Lug Pass in the Bavarian Alps, he found an industrious salt mining community at the site of ancient Juvavum, Salzburg, where the primeval forest had encroached on nearly all of the famed community laid waste during the Germanic invasions. Here Rupert "Apostle to the Bavarians" founded a monastery and added new life to the community which was to be the seat of the bishopric and of the later diocese of Salzburg.

He founded St. Peter's Church, where he later was buried, and established a convent on the Nonnenberg.

Legend has it that he converted Duke Theodo of Bavaria, and baptized him and his retainers. To make the best of his opportunity and weaken the influence of his Frank overlord, he liberally patronized Rupert by permitting him to travel about the country, to build churches and to teach the people. The ducal castle, overlooking the site of the church, and the lands adjoining the castle were placed at the disposal of Rupert. The mountain guarding the Lug Pass was transformed. A residence for the parish priests was built near St. Peter's. Building activity directly associated with the evolving church community attracted artisans of many skills, and Salzburg soon became a focal point for Christian endeavor.

For the support of this ambitious venture Rupert received one tenth of all the salt processed in the vicinity of Salzburg, the right to collect tolls at the Lug, and fifty Roman slaves. Monasteries and convents planted in six outlying hamlets were endowed with lands and vineyards. At the filial monasteries of the mother church resident monks were permitted to perform certain religious rites. The Salzburg Benedictine monastery, over which Rupert presided, was made a training school for priests.[4] But not until after his death was Salzburg made a bishopric by Boniface.

Anglo-Saxon Winfred, given the name Boniface by the Pope in 719, did more than any other person to convert the pagan Germans and to bring about religious unity and administrative centralization in the Roman church of Europe. Quite early in his career he recognized the Pope as the spiritual head of Christendom. In 718, when in Rome, he was given a mandate by the Pope to work among the Germans. Five years later Charles Martel appointed him Archbishop of Mainz and primate of Germany, an office which he held until 754. After 739, as papal legate, he was instructed to bend his efforts toward the organization of the church in Bavaria.

The Duke of Bavaria authorized Boniface to set the boundary for the diocese of Salzburg, Passau, Regensburg, and Freising. At

---

[4]Widmann, *Geschichte Salzburgs*, V. I, p. 62, discounts much of what has been ascribed to Rupert. According to the author, Virgil, successor to Rupert in 767, many years after Rupert's death, to complete the historical record of the Salzburg diocese, left the account. In the words of Widmann, the stories of the lives of saints are the most controversial of medieval literature.

the insistence of Duke Odilo, whose demand the Pope could not deny, Boniface laid the foundation for a national Bavarian church. John, probably an English associate of Boniface, was appointed as the first Bishop of Salzburg with the approval of the Duke of Bavaria (739-745). At the same time he held the office of abbot of the Benedictine monastery.

The dual office of abbot and bishop gave him an enviable place among his colleagues, for in most instances the two offices were held separately. The princes, therefore, as they looked with increasing apprehension upon the mounting influence and power of the bishops, used the abbots as makeweights against them. Whether directly under the thumb of the princes or not, the abbots found in such an alliance a means for escape from the ambitious jurisdictional claims of a bishop. In the diocese of Salzburg the bishop exercised all of the functions appertaining to that office throughout his diocese, and as abbot he was the administrative and spiritual supervisor over the monks of the chapter, and over all of the monastic estates, its tenants, serfs, and slaves.

CHAPTER III

FROM BISHOPRIC TO ARCHBISHOPRIC
(750-914)

To A considerable degree the rise of Salzburg to prominence in Germany was stimulated by the struggle for power between the Bavarian dukes and the kings of the Franks. Each contender sought the support of the bishop of Salzburg through liberal grants of land and privileges.

While Pepin II was preoccupied, Odilo, a vassal to Pepin II, consolidated his hold upon Bavaria. Not only did he negotiate alliances with neighboring stem-dukes, but to that end secured the tacit approval of the pope, whose chief concern was the recognition of himself as the spiritual head of the Bavarian church. All of this posed a real menace to Carolingian imperialism. In the war that followed, Pepin II defeated the Bavarian forces and captured Odilo. During the latter's brief term of imprisonment in the royal castle his duchy was governed by the Franks. In 744, after the loss of a sizeable part of his patrimonial holdings, Odilo, Pepin's brother-in-law, was restored to his duchy. His son, Tassilo, who succeeded to the office four years later, violated his oath of allegiance by proclaiming his independence of the Franks.

By 772, Tassilo had reached the zenith of his power. His marital relationship with the Lombard dynasty in northern Italy and the Benevento family in the southern part of the peninsula was a diplomatic victory Charlemagne (768-814), king of the Franks, could hardly ignore. With the blessing of the church of Bavaria, Tassilo had himself proclaimed the "New Constantine." For fifteen years, while Charlemagne was engaged in wars against the Saxons in the east and the Saracens in the west, the "New Constantine" strengthened his position. In 787, the ruler of the Franks decided to put an end to Tassilo's ambitious program. The would-be "Constantine" was forced by Charlemagne to surrender his patrimony and swear allegiance to the emperor. In return his duchy was restored to him as a fief from Charlemagne. But he hastened his undoing through an alliance with the Lombards of Italy. Following the defeat of the allies in 788, Tassilo was tried by the imperial diet and convicted as a traitor. His execution was commuted by Charlemagne on condition that he take a monastic vow and reside in a monastery for the remainder of his life.

The stem-duchy of Bavaria was incorporated into the Frankish empire, but its political entity remained intact. Charlemagne's brother-in-law was made prefect of the conquered state. The Bavarian church was incorporated into the diocese of the Bishop of Salzburg.

The fight for power within the empire enabled the restive Slavs along its eastern border, extending from the Baltic toward the Adriatic, to advance westward. Toward the south they had pushed up along the Danube and its tributaries into the Alpine region. The Slavic Avars were temporarily halted by Charlemagne in 797, and were incorporated into a buffer state called the Pannonian March. To assist in their cultural assimilation, Germans were colonized in the newly created march. The bishop of Salzburg was directed to minister to the spiritual needs of the colonists and to convert the pagan Slavs. To guard against further attack, the defenses of the monasteries and of the bishoprics of Salzburg and Passau in Bavaria were strengthened.

Recognizing the importance of Salzburg, the kings of the Franks saw to the elevation of able men to the office of bishop. One of the ablest of them was Virgil, 745-784, successor to John, the first bishop. Virgil was born and reared in Ireland in the tradition of the Celtic church, and had risen to the rank of abbot in his native land. In 743 we find him at the court of the Mayor of the Palace, where he was highly regarded for his scholarly attainments and administrative ability. At court he met Odilo, Duke of Bavaria, then a prisoner of Pepin II. In the year following Odilo's restoration to the duchy in 745, Pepin II, with the approval of the Duke of Bavaria, had Virgil appointed bishop of Salzburg. Like other Celtic churchmen, he refused canonical consecration by a Roman prelate. He did, however, assume all of the functions of his office except those reserved exclusively to a bishop under the canon law. These were exercised by a regional Scottish bishop.

He emulated the sainted Rupert, who had laid the foundation for the Salzburg bishopric. It is to his honor that he commenced the building of St. Peter's, in the City of Salzburg, a church which was not completed until the thirteenth century. At its dedication in 774 the ashes of Rupert, its patron saint, were entombed in the cathedral. Then, at the request of his parishioners and the diocesan clergy, Virgil broke with the Celtic tradition to accept canonical consecration.

He resolutely held out against anything that ran contrary to his deep convlctions. Neither Boniface nor the Duke of Bavaria could persuade him to give ground in matters of conscience. Virgil resisted every effort of the duke to found a monastery free of the jurisdiction of the bishop. Only after his authority over it was recognized as inviolable was it established. In a controversy with Boniface, papal legate in Germany, in which Virgil denied the validity of baptism when administered by an unlearned priest, he was upheld by Pope Zacharias. He did not hesitate to challenge certain doctrines of Isidore of Seville and the Venerable Bede, both recognized authorities of the church. Contrary to their doctrine, he believed in and publicly announced his belief in the existence of antipodes, people or countries to be found on directly opposite sides of the earth. Boniface was shocked by his theory and condemned as a heresy the claim that another world of people existed down under and that the sun and moon shone upon these antipodes. That anyone should deign to teach "that another world existed not redeemed by Christ" was so revolting to Pope Zacharias he ordered Virgil to be sent to Rome for trial at the papal court. Whether the order was carried out or not is not known. We do know that he was duly consecrated as bishop of Salzburg, an office which he held until his death in 784.

Following a short interval after the death of Virgil, when the affairs of the diocese were administered by the abbot of St. Peter's, the emperor appointed Arn (785-821) to the office of bishop. He was a statesman of exceptional ability and highly regarded by the emperor. The abbot of St. Denis was sent to Rome by Charlemagne to notify Pope Leo III of the appointment. At the request of the emperor, the pontiff vested Arn with the pallium, the official cloak of a bishop. In 811, Arn with eleven other clerical dignitaries was honored at Aachen by being privileged to witness Charlemagne's signature to his last will and testament. Under him Salzburg was raised to the rank of archdiocese. At the same time, Charlemagne elevated him to be primate of the Bavarian church, and Salzburg became the focal point of religious matters in southeastern Germany.

Arn, a Bavarian, was as prominent in the counsels of Tassilo III (748-788), Duke of Bavaria, as in those of Charlemagne. For that very reason, Tassilo considered him the logical person to represent the duke at the imperial court at Aachen. Under his administration, a survey was made of all the lands with which the bishop had been endowed. By royal authorization he was permitted to exchange more remote lands for holdings more contiguous to Salzburg. He was as firm as his predecessor in maintaining his jurisdiction over every new monastery founded within the rapidly expanding diocese. By stressing beauty rather than utility in the construction of churches and monasteries he showed the influence of the architecture of Aachen.

The education and training of priests and missionaries was a matter of utmost concern to Arn. For guidance he looked to Alcuin, the founder of Charlemagne's Palace School. Students from Salzburg were sent to Tours, a famous western educational center which had been established by Alcuin. Two scholars of the Palace School were employed to teach at the seat of the bishopric. For an understanding of the "mystical numbers of the Bible" the study of mathematics was stressed. Books to be copied by the scribes of the Salzburg diocesan monasteries were furnished by Alcuin, and he made an outright gift of one hundred and fifty volumes to the diocesan library, one of which is extant, and on exhibit in that city.

The age of Charlemagne was one during which the new languages that had evolved subsequent to the barbarian invasions of the fifth century were crystallizing. Latinized languages were spoken in ancient Gaul and Italy, Germanic speech east of the Rhine, and Slavic tongues farther to the east and southeast. To cope with such a problem Alcuin sent Adelbert, a scholar and able linguist, from the Palace School to teach at Salzburg. As an interpreter for the French scholar, Wito, Adelbert laid the foundation for German theological education at Arn's school.

Charlemagne affirmed to Arn all grants and privileges which had been bestowed upon the diocese. By a general decree, immunity was extended to all bishoprics of the empire, and through it the Salzburg diocese obtained a clear title to its lands, its people, and everything on the lands as well as exemption from imperial taxes. All offences committed therein, except those pertaining to life and limb, were to be tried in the court of the diocese, and it had claim to the fine assessed against an offender. In a powerful state like Bavaria, immunity and royal protection were exceedingly valuable to the church as well as to the emperor.

Arn was entrusted with the conversion of the Avars, a Slavic tribe, after they had been conquered by Charlemagne in 706. The colonization of their lands by Germans was probably begun soon thereafter, and the fortifications of the bishopric of Salzburg, of those of Passau, and of the convents of Bavaria were strengthened to withstand Slavic attacks. The Bavarian church was formed into a diocese to be administered by an archbishop, and Arn was designated by the emperor for the office. At the behest of Charlemagne Abbot Fardulf of St. Denis, a skilled diplomat, was instructed to notify Pope Leo III of his action. To this the Pope readily acceded by appointing Arn archbishop of Salzburg and head of the church of Bavaria.

By no stretch of the imagination could the place at the Lug Pass, Salzburg, be called a city. Hard by the Moenchsberg was St. Peter's monastery and chapel, the residence of the bishop and of the diocesan officials. In all probability, persons closely associated with the church, artisans, freemen, and even merchants must have resided along the narrow streets of the inner city, still there in the Salzburg of today. The street names Juden, Gold, Siegmund, Haffner, Getreidegasse (Grain Street) and the like are clues to the occupation or character of their residents. St. Michael's Church of the inner city, near the present café *Glockenspiel,* dates back to 800. It was rebuilt in the second half of the eighteenth century and had probably been a parish church and community center.

CHAPTER IV

FROM ARCHBISHOPRIC TO PRINCE-ARCHBISHOPRIC
(914-1250)

THE REMAINS of Charlemagne had hardly been entombed at Aachen in 814, when the vast structure he had built collapsed. For more than two centuries, European society and with it the empire drifted toward a state of feudal anarchy. Beset by hostile Northmen, Slavs, Hungarians, and Saracens all along its border, broken up into separate cultural and geographical sections, not even a person of Charlemagne's stature could have stemmed the tide of disintegration.[1] This and the absence of a fixed system of succession to the imperial throne made for a state of confusion from which Europe was not to recover for four centuries.

The agreement reached by Charlemagne's grandsons, whereby the Empire was divided into three parts, merely recognized the linguistic changes which had occurred in the Empire since the Germanic invasions. In 843 the grandsons agreed to the division of the Empire. Louis the German was recognized as king of the Germans and was accorded the territory east of the Rhine. Charles the Bald received the French territory west of the Scheldt and the Meuse. Lothair, who held the title of Emperor, was given the central strip between the territory which lay between the territory of his brothers and Italy. Following his death in 870, his brothers divided Lorraine, the central strip between them. Until recent years this area has been a bone of contention between Germany and France.[2]

---

[1]These disastrous events are vividly described by contemporary chroniclers quoted in Thompson and Johnson, *An Introduction to Medieval Europe*, p. 263: "Cities are depopulated, the monasteries ruined and burned, the country reduced to solitude. . . . Every man does what seems good in his eye. . . . The strong oppress the weak, the world is full of violence against the poor and the plunder of ecclesiastical goods. . . . Men devour one another like fishes in the sea."

[2]Ruth Putnam, in *Alsace Lorraine or From Caesar to Kaiser*, describes this conflict.

The separatist trends in the kingdom of Louis the German and the aspirations of the stem-duke of Bavaria in no way lessened the zeal of the Salzburg prelates for missionary activity among the Slavs. In 824, Adalram, probably a Bavarian and an accomplished linguist, succeeded Archbishop Arn, and held that office to 836. He had been first heard of as archdeacon of the diocese of Salzburg. He and others after him were but slightly concerned with affairs of the empire, particularly with the conflict between Louis the Pious and his three sons. They were, however, zealous in encouraging missionary endeavor among the Slavs. Adalram visited the Moravian Slavic marches regularly. Through his efforts the Slavs of Bavaria and the Moravians of the East March,[3] later called Austria, were brought into an affiliation with the Roman church. For the support of this ambitious program the later archbishop Liuphramm received extensive grants of land in the East March. Under his directives, masons, carpenters, painters, and blacksmiths were sent to Moravia to have a hand in the construction of houses of worship and thus further the economic advance of the expanding Christian communities.

Western Christian missionaries in lands occupied by the Slavs soon encountered others sent by the Christians of Constantinople. This bastion alone had successfully held out against the menacing advance of the Saracens in the ninth century. To safeguard its western approach the Christians of Constantinople bent their energy toward the conversion of the Slavs and other barbarians in southeastern Europe. Though eastern and western Christendom had not yet separated, keen competition between the two sets of missionaries soon developed. Most active of the easterners were Methodius and Constantine, sons of a Greek father of Thessalonika. Both were accomplished Slavic linguists. These had a decided propaganda advantage over their Western rivals, for the Slavs were distrustful of the imperialist designs of the Roman church. Not restricted to a ritualistic language, the missionaries from the East adopted the language of the people in all religious services. To overcome this

---

[3]The Moravian marches had been established by Charlemagne along the Waag and the March, both tributaries of the Danube. The German name for the March was Marave, hence the name Maehren, in English Moravia. The two were later consolidated into the East March, German *Ost Mark* later *Ostreich* or *Oesterreich* (Austria).

handicap the Roman Pope Hadrian II (862-872) authorized the use of the mother tongue in the religious services of the Slavs.

This innovation precipitated a bitter controversy among the pro-Slav and the anti-Slav churchmen in Bavaria. To resolve the matter, the archbishop of Salzburg and primate of Bavaria ordered a synodical meeting of the higher clergy of his diocese. In the course of the debates, tempers flared. In a fit of anger an anti-Slav ritualist lashed out, struck his opponent, and accused him of wanting to sever the tie of fellowship between the Moravian and the Bavarian church. The conflict which lingered on came to an end when the Hungarians invaded the East March and occupied Moravia in 905-906. For many years thereafter, the missionary endeavor of Salzburg was limited to the valley of the Enns River and the region of the Alps.

Following the division of the Empire in the Mersen agreement of 870, Louis the German looked to Salzburg as a makeweight to the separatist designs of the stem-duke of Bavaria. In 874, following his appointment of Theotmar to the seat of the episcopate (874-907), Louis bestowed upon him the title of royal chaplain and lord high chancellor. When the capital of the German kingdom was transferred from Frankfurt to Regensburg, Theotmar displaced the archbishop of Mainz as German primate. From then until his death on the field of battle against the Hungarians in 906, Theotmar had an active part in the political and diplomatic affairs of Germany.

The inability of the German king to cope with the mounting enemy pressure along the eastern border compelled the affected princes to meet this hostile advance alone. In the battle of Pressburg in 906, the Duke of Bavaria and his feudal allies were decisively defeated. The flower of Bavarian nobility, including the duke and Theotmar, archbishop of Salzburg, lay dead on the field of battle. This, the most catastrophic war in the annals of Salzburg history, wiped out the cultural fruits of more than a century, and Salzburg lost its spiritual hold on the mid-Danubian region. It reverted to the status of a Bavarian bishopric, and for many years was obliged to concern itself with the task of economic reconstruction.

Again the Archbishop of Salzburg became a vassal to the Bavarian duke. His authority over the archbishop was confirmed by Conrad of Franconia, who in 911 was chosen king by the north

German princes to succeed the last of the Carolingian line, Louis the Child. Conrad, to obtain the support of the Duke of Bavaria, relinquished to him the authority to appoint the archbishop of Salzburg and the primate of the church of Bavaria.

An ambitious archbishop who had enjoyed many of the privileges of a temporal prince could hardly be expected to stand by and calmly accept the loss of prestige involved in ducal rather than royal appointment. The Duke of Bavaria, Arnulf, whose father had lost his life at Pressburg, was determined to assert his independence of the king, and so the prelate of Salzburg readily made the best of any pretext for ridding himself of ducal overlordship.

In the fight for survival against the Hungarian Magyars, Duke Arnulf found it necessary to confiscate church lands with which to reward the newly recruited knights who assisted in repelling the enemy. His military success and consequent public acclaim promted him to defy royal authority and proclaim himself "Archduke" (Herzog) by the "Grace of God." In response to such a challenge, Conrad, the German king, and his ally, Archbishop Pilgrim of Salzburg, joined forces against Duke Arnulf "in the name of Christianity and the Church." The duke's lands were devastated by the enemy and he sought temporary asylum with the Magyars, who were then at peace with Bavaria. In 916, however, when the tide of events turned against King Conrad, Arnulf returned and, when it became necessary for him to appoint a successor to the deceased Pilgrim, he cast aside all thoughts of canonical qualification. For the archbishopric he selected a titled nobleman Odelbert. The latter, to meet the requirement of celibacy, set aside his wife, who had borne him two sons, who held the title of count (Graf), and three daughters. In return for the transfer of several benefices to his wife, he exacted of her a pledge of celibacy for the remainder of her life. Odelbert's chief concern was the economic improvement of Salzburg.

The stem-ducal aspiration for local autonomy was challenged by Henry I of Saxony, chosen in 919 to succeed Conrad as king. Henry, having defeated the aggressors along the border, seemed the logical leader to save Germany from military disaster. Secure from invasions, Henry gave attention to the consolidation of his position in Germany. He was successful in winning the support of the burgher class and the higher clergy against their respective rulers. For they were as jealous of their prerogatives and as opposed to encroachment of their princes upon their powers as the princes were hostile toward the expansion of the king's prerogatives at their expense. Henry and his successors endowed the churchmen with lands and granted charters and certain imperial rights to towns to free them of interference by their princes. In time, many towns received charters of incorporation from the king and several of the more important archdioceses like Trier, Worms, and Salzburg were made independent principalities.

Under Otto I (936-973), the son and successor to Henry I, the archbishop of Salzburg again assumed an important place in the king's council. In 939, Otto ordered the appointment of Heroldt, Duke Arnulf's nephew, to the episcopate (939-958). Thereafter the archbishop was frequently seen at the royal court and was accorded the honor of having bestowed upon him the title of royal chaplain and lord high chancellor of the realm. In 945, the previously held immunities were restored, and the ducal jurisdiction over his lands and the freemen was transferred to the archbishop. To assure his loyalty, Otto endowed the bishop with lands and vineyards. A vineyard, on the slope of the *Sausal,* is to this day the source of a well-known regional wine. To increase his holdings, Heroldt forged titles to lands to which he had no claim, a practice not uncommon among medieval churchmen. For who was there to challenge the churchmen at a time when they had a monopoly of learning?

When Otto was again faced with the efforts of the stem-dukes to overthrow the royal power at a time when he was plagued by Hungarian invasions (951-955), Heroldt broke with his benefactor by joining the enemy. Following the decisive defeat of the Hungarians at Lechfeld and the siege of Regensburg (955), Heroldt was captured and ordered to be blinded and sent into exile by Otto I. Many of his holdings were transferred to allies of the king of Germany. In response to a request of the king of Germany, the blinded prelate was excommunicated by the pope for his heretical and rebellious conduct.

Three years after the deposition of Heroldt Otto appointed Frederick, Count of Chiemgau (961-991), to the episcopate of Salzburg. The new churchman proved himself a staunch supporter of the cause of church reform as advocated by the Benedictine monks of Cluny in Burgundy at the opening of the tenth century.

Like the Cluny congregation he was firm in his fight against such evils as simony, the sale of church offices by laymen, lay investiture, a practice by which a non-churchman, such as a king, would dare to invest the clergy with spiritual authority, and the marriage of the clergy. With Slavic affairs again stabilized, Frederick was able to resume spiritual supervision of the Bavarian Slavs and those nearby. Under him the Moravians were returned to the Salzburg fold, and houses of worship that had been wrecked by the Magyar invasion were rebuilt.

The loyalty of Frederick and his successors was liberally rewarded by Otto I[4] and subsequent German rulers. In 996, Otto III granted the archbishop of Salzburg the right of coinage. Emperor Conrad II (1024-1039) endowed Archbishop Theotmar II (1025-1041) with game and forest lands in the valley of the Inn and the Salzach. Pope John XIX bestowed the pallium upon him, and allowed him to be preceded in processions by one bearing a cross and to be seated on a mount covered with a scarlet blanket. In case of the absence of a papal legate at Salzburg for the publication of an official decree from Rome, the archbishop himself was to act in that capacity.

In the course of the struggle for power in Germany between the imperialist Ghibellines of Swabia and the anti-imperialist Guelfs of Bavaria, which lasted from the twelfth well into the thirteenth century, the Archbishop of Salzburg successfully maintained his balance on the tight rope of diplomacy. In the early encounters the Ghibellines were led by Henry (the Lion) of Bavaria, and the Guelfs by the picturesque and able Frederick I, known also as Frederick Barbarossa (Red Beard). Following his defeat in 1180 by Barbarossa, Henry the Lion was deposed and shorn of his holdings in Bavaria and Saxony. These were parceled out to the supporters of Emperor Frederick I. Salzburg was separated from Bavaria and made into an independent principality of the Empire and the burghers of the city were accorded a corporate charter, thus assuring the emperor safer passage from the Danube to Italy.

---

[4]In 962 Otto I was crowned Roman Emperor by the pope. In the thirteenth century Otto's lands became known as the Holy Roman Empire, of which Voltaire later said, that it was not holy, or Roman, or an Empire.

When the successors of Frederick Barbarossa, Henry VI and his son Frederick II, resisted the Pope's determination to abolish lay investiture we find Count Eberhard II of Regensburg, who was also Archbishop of Salzburg 1200-1246, on the side of the Emperor. He remained steadfast in that support in the face of the ban of excommunication imposed on Frederick II when he refused to accede to the papal demand that he go on a crusade. Unable to rid himself of this obstructionist, the Pope placed all communities including Salzburg, which remained loyal to the emperor, under the interdict. In spite of this suspension of all religious rights except baptism and extreme unction in Archbishop Eberhard's principality of Salzburg, he remained loyal to his sovereign until his death in 1246. As a last resort the Pope excommunicated Eberhard II, and because of his refusal to repent he was buried in an unconsecrated vault outside the city of Rastadt. Not until 42 years later were his ashes permitted to be interred in the diocesan cathedral in Salzburg.

At the time of the Interregnum (1254-1273), when Germany was without an emperor, Salzburg to all intents and purposes was an independent state. In 1273, when Rudolph, the first of the Hapsburgs of Austria, was elected emperor the archbishopric was in name only a fief of the German Empire.

In spite of violent political and ecclesiastical controversies in Germany, the cultural revival in Salzburg was not seriously interrupted. The churchmen who were entrusted with its destiny in the transition from the late medieval era to the era of the Renaissance were men of ability. Emperor Conrad, in 1149, stated publicly that nowhere in Germany were clericals to be found who merited public respect more than those of Salzburg.

The upsurge of learning in the bishopric was stimulated by scholars from the monastery of St. Gall, the cultural beacon light on Lake Constance. Much as Arn of Salzburg had looked to Aachen and the Palace School of Alcuin in the ninth and tenth century, so his successors of the eleventh and twelfth looked to the monastery of St. Gall. Wooden religious structures destroyed by fire were replaced by more permanent ones of masonry. Though all traces of St. Virgil's Cathedral itself have disappeared, survivals of frescoes, busts, artistic decorations and sacramental vessels afford visual evidences of the skilled craftsmanship and artistic know-how of its builders. Undoubtedly, one of the most precious works of the Salzburg craftsmen is the silver tray which was unearthed at Werfen by a railroad construction crew in 1874, now on exhibit at the Salzburg museum. In it engraved in relief is the bust of an archbishop bearing the inscription *Titmarus Archepiscopus Salisburganis.*

CHAPTER V

SALZBURG IN TRANSITION
(1273-1496)

MEDIEVAL civilization had reached its height in the thirteenth century. Further progress of a Christian civilization erected upon an ancient foundation was no longer possible. The higher clergy and the nobility who had intrenched themselves in the so-called Holy Roman Empire fought desperately to stem the tidal wave of change in the fourteenth and fifteenth centuries. The concept of an empire in which matters political were administered by an emperor, and spiritual affairs by the Pope in Rome, of necessity had to give way to the impact of a changing social and political order. National states, each with a characteristic culture, defied the concept of universality. The evolution of folk songs, national plays, the emergence of a vernacular literature, and the translation of the Bible into the language of the layman were all parts of the new order. Old cities were revitalized and new commercial and industrial centers reborn, and laymen began to challenge the intellectual monopoly enjoyed by the clergy of the Middle Ages.

It was in such an atmosphere fraught with international rivalry and diplomatic intrigue that Renaissance Salzburg found itself involved. The spiritual and political life of the prince-archbishopric during the Interregnum (1256-1273) was such as to defy analysis. The demoralized character of the higher clergy was a fair reflection of that of the rank and file of churchmen. The episcopate was subjected to a succession of papal appointees none of whom was worthy of the dignity of that office. Resentful of the usurpation of its elective prerogative, the Salzburg cathedral chapter, after the sudden death of Archbishop Wladislaus, made haste in 1270 to take advantage of a papal crisis by appointing Frederick II von Walchen (1270-1284).

For years the archbishopric of Salzburg had been a bone of contention between Bavaria and Austria. By 1270, Ottokar II, king of Bohemia, was set to promote his cause in Salzburg after having annexed Kaernten and other small principalities to the south of that town. Had it not been for the keen rivalry of its three neighbors and in particular the contention for the German imperial throne by Ottokar and the Archduke of Austria, Salzburg might have succumbed. For the vassals of the archbishop were sullen and in a rebellious mood. A part of the city had been destroyed by fire, and famine was stalking in the community. The diocese was burdened with debt, and much of the bishop's patrimony had been alienated. Distress in the Hallein salt works, the most lucrative of Salzburg's industries and sources of revenue for the archbishop, was climaxed by a workers' strike in 1276. Had it been successful, the tottering economy of Salzburg might have collapsed.

Frederick II, prince-bishop of Salzburg, was admirably qualified for bringing order to the confused economic, political, and international situation within the principality. He proved himself a shrewd diplomat. A contemporary historian declared him to have been one of the most farsighted and cunning men of his time, and that in him Ottokar II of Bohemia had found his master. In 1272 Frederick set out for Rome to secure the pallium from the Pope. But the Holy See, before awarding him the official insignia of office, insisted that he pay the loan made to Salzburg by merchants of Rome and Siena. The following year Frederick II entered into a secret alliance with Rudolph I of Austria, the newly elected German emperor, against the latter's most powerful enemy, Ottokar II of Bohemia.

Sensing the secret maneuvers of Frederick II to enlist allies for Rudolph of Austria,[1] Ottokar decided to act before the emperor had time to consolidate his position and come to the support of his ally, Frederick II. Ottokar therefore called upon Frederick II to attend a meeting of his vassals at Prague, the

---

[1] In Gebhardt, *Handbuch der Deutschen Geschichte* I., p. 390. The bishop of Basel is quoted as saying when he heard of Rudolph's election: "Lord God, hold on to your throne lest Rudolph unseat you." According to Gebhardt, the Emperor had distinguished himself as a brave fighter and military strategist, a frugal and wise administrator, an experienced and objective politician whose sincere and simple life won him the confidence of his associates. He was careful not to arouse suspicion of himself among the German electors, who considered him well qualified to bring peace and justice to a Germany faced by **anarchy.**

capital of Bohemia. The summons was ignored by the archbishop until he found the Emperor unwilling to come to his aid against Ottokar II. When the Bohemian king demanded that Frederick II refuse to support the Emperor in an offensive against Bohemia, Frederick II quit the conclave and returned to Salzburg.

The vicious attack by Ottokar on Salzburg was not long in coming. Neither the Emperor nor the Pope was in a position to come to the aid of Archbishop Frederick II. He was treated to the spectacle of having his unfortified towns and hamlets put to the torch. Fortified towns were stormed, looted, and set afire Hundreds of worshipers who had sought refuge in churches perished in flames. Only a few fortresses held out against the enemy. Expediency dictated to Frederick II the wisdom of submitting to the humiliating terms of the conqueror; however, he secretly assured the Emperor that he would keep faith with him.

Undismayed by the disastrous consequences of war, Frederick II, almost immediately after his defeat, set out to seek out allies for Rudolph and himself against the King of Bohemia. The Duke of Bavaria, who was kindly disposed toward Rudolf, entered into an alliance when Frederick II agreed to recognize the duke's territorial claims in Salzburg. As soon as other alliances had been negotiated successfully a three-pronged attack was launched against Bohemia which resulted in victory for the allies. In return for his military assistance and the losses suffered at the hands of Ottokar, Frederick II was permitted to keep much of the loot of war, and his title was confirmed to the right of collecting tolls at the bridge crossing the Salzach at the Lug Pass. The Archbishop of Salzburg had now become the most prominent prelate in south Germany. For the five years of the Emperor's residence at Vienna, the archbishop was zealous in promoting the interests of the Hapsburgs. An imperial decree of 1277 accorded to him the rights, privileges, and regalia of a prince of the empire and the right to sit in judgment at civil and criminal trials in his state.

Frederick II soon brought order out of the chaos in Salzburg inherited from the Interregnum and the destruction at the hands of Ottokar. His restive vassals were brought under control, and he dealt successfully with the ills which were responsible for the class struggle in Salzburg. By the time of his death, April 7, 1284, he had carved an honored niche for himself in the history of his bishopric. A contemporary said of him that he was pious and patient and through modest manner and the help of God he advanced the welfare of the church.

Almost immediately upon the death of Archbishop Frederick II the Emperor of Germany, Rudolph I, made haste to have his own candidate chosen by the cathedral chapter of Salzburg, thus depriving the Pope of the lucrative privilege of nomination. To assure himself of one beholden to him, Rudolph broke with the customary practice of appointing a member of the higher nobility. He designated Rudolph of Hohenegg, a person of humble Swabian knighthood, who had served him as chancellor and vicar of the realm. Preoccupied with the pressing problems of his diocese, Rudolph, Archbishop of Salzburg (1284-1290), sent his personal representative to Rome to have Pope Honorius IV bestow the pallium. The grant was postponed, pending the payment of a debt by the cathedral chapter which had been incurred by a previous archbishop with the bankers of Florence.

The death of Rudolph of Salzburg in 1290 and that of Rudolph I of Hapsburg, the German emperor, a year later, was disastrous for Salzburg. Like vultures its neighbors sought to control the rich prize. Rival candidates were proposed to the Pope. His appointment of Conrad of Levant (1291-1312) was opposed both by the cathedral chapter and by the Duke of Bavaria. In the war which soon followed, between Bavaria and Austria, Conrad fought on the side of Austria. Throughout his career as prince-bishop of Salzburg Conrad played an important role in the competition of the Austrian and Bavarian houses for the imperial throne.

From 1290 to 1365, when Pilgrim II was consecrated to the office of bishop, Salzburg politics were deeply enmeshed in the Austro-Bavarian contest for the German imperial title. As though this were not enough, the troubled events within the Empire were further complicated by the "Babylonian Captivity" of the Church (1308-1378), and the subsequent Great Schism (1378-1414).[2] The only archbishop of any stature in this confused

---

[2]In 1308 Clement V, a Frenchman, transferred his residence from Rome to Avignon for national and security reasons and to escape the factional conflicts in Rome. This so-called Babylonian Captivity of the church (1308-1378) was followed by the Great Schism (1378-1414) when there were two Popes, one in Rome and the other at Avignon, each claiming to be the Vicar of Christ. The Council of Pisa called to

epoch was Frederick III (1315-1398) who was appointed by the chapter of Salzburg and obtained the pallium from the Pope at Avignon. Like so many of his predecessors, he was a statesman and warrior rather than a spiritual leader. He was well educated, and did much in the years of his term of office to restore the territorial autonomy of the prince-archbishop.

For more than twenty years after Frederick III's death, factional strife divided the cathedral chapter of Salzburg into two hostile camps. In 1365, each faction elected its own candidate. The elections were annulled by Pope Urban V, who then appointed Pilgrim II (1365-1396), the favored choice of the Austrian majority faction in the chapter. The appointee himself was a typical Renaissance personality from a proud and influential Austrian family. He was shrewd, resolute, generally unyielding, and devoid of conscious scruples when his own selfish interest was concerned, regardless of affairs of the Empire or the Church. He was careful not to break openly with either of the rival popes, and only swerved from his obstinate determination when it was apparent to him that a firm stand would get him nothing.

Pilgrim spent lavishly to satisfy a craving for a place of distinction among the princes of the Empire. He left no stone unturned to regain the coveted title of Imperial Chaplain. Despite his faults, his success in the field of diplomacy, trade, finance, and law, and as patron of art and learning placed him in the vanguard of Salzburg statesmen.

The Duke of Bavaria, who sensed an alliance of Pilgrim with his enemy the league of Swabian cities, in 1387 demanded an accounting of the prince-archbishop. When Pilgrim and his thirty-four retainers appeared at court, they were made prisoners. This treacherous act kindled resentment in all of Salzburg. Its guildsmen organized themselves into a political corporation and emergency governments were established throughout the archbishopric by diocesan bishops, judges, and burgomasters of the

---

put an end to the complicated situation by appointing John XXIII. The other two refused to recognize the authority of the council and refused to abdicate. The factional conflict was a menace to the political and religious structure of western Christendom. In many instances two and three bishops appointed by rival Popes laid claim to the same office. Is it any wonder that an Italian wit remarked: "One Pope for each member of the Trinity"? The Schism was ended by the Council of Constance summoned by Emperor Sigismund 1414.

towns, and measures were adopted to force the release of the detained victims. The ban of excommunication upon Frederick of Bavaria by the Salzburg cathedral chapter and Pope Urban's appeal to the emperor were followed by their release.

The territorial consolidation of Salzburg was carried out by Eberhard III, who succeeded Pilgrim in 1396. The archbishopric as a united territorial state was made subject to the personal jurisdiction of the archbishop. Toward the close of the century the territory north and west of the city was brought under the immediate jurisdiction of Salzburg.

In the century after Pilgrim II, a period of almost uninterrupted economic and spiritual decline was experienced. No fewer than eleven bishops followed in rapid succession. On the whole, their influence in matters pertaining to the empire was slight, but in a general way they supported Austrian imperialism.

CHAPTER VI

ECONOMIC, SOCIAL, AND RELIGIOUS TRENDS
(1273-1496)

MAN AND BEAST must have been attracted to the salt outcroppings of Salzburg long before the chronicler made mention of them: There seems little doubt that salt-mining had been carried on since prehistoric times at Hallein and the Duerrnberg, a fifteen-minute drive over the Austrian Alpine road from Salzburg. The mining tools of the Celts attest to the existence of this industry at Hallein more than 3000 years ago. In recognition of the importance of this most essential resource, the Bavarians, when they invaded the Roman Empire, named the river which flows through the region the Salzach. The Berchtesgaden deposits first mentioned in 1194 must have been worked long before.

A tour of this oldest mine of central Europe, with shafts about 1500 feet below the ground, is an unforgettable event of anyone's life. Clad in miner's garb, led by a guide lighting the path, one trudges through long mine caverns, down a steep stairway (75-100 steps), shoots down five slides at about a 45 degree angle for distances ranging from 140 to 400 feet. In the course of the tour a crystal clear, well illuminated salt lake eight to ten feet deep is crossed, and the thrilling experience comes to an end after riding astride a rail conveyance *Grubenhund* (mine express) for a distance of about two and one-half miles when one again emerges into the light of day, after an adventure of about 90 minutes. In the underground tour one crosses the border from Austria to Berchtesgaden in Germany twice. Here at Hallein is the tomb of Franz Xaver Gruber, who, inspired by the reverent atmosphere and hallowed silence of this quaint community, composed "Silent Night, Holy Night."

A method for mining the salt deposits may have been suggested by the already-developed gold mining industry. Mine shafts supported by wooden props were hewn into the mountain. Pits were then carved into the mass of rock salt and flooded with fresh water. When the water had been saturated with salt, it was drained through conduits down the side of the mountain to evaporation huts accessible to means of transportation. The most numerous of the laborers in the industry were the men who harvested and split the vast quantity of firewood necessary for the removal of water through evaporation. The salt was finally packed into tubs and casks for shipment. To this day much the same process is pursued for extracting the salt deposits in the Duerrnberg. Two pipe lines extend along the mine tunnel, one carrying fresh water to the lake and the other conveying back the brine to the evaporation plant at the Salzach, now the center of a thriving chemical and industrial community.

Originally, the proprietorship of a certain number of brine receptacles or evaporation pans was held by the ruling prince, the cathedral chapter, the monastic orders, and the Goldecker family. Toward the end of the thirteenth century the Archbishop of Salzburg began liquidating the holdings of his competitors, and by 1350 had made himself sole owner of the industry. About a century later he had monopolized the salt trade which had been carried on by the burghers. Is it any wonder that resentment and a rebellious spirit mounted against the prince-archbishop, who had a monopoly of the "Bread of Life" and the salt so necessary for sustaining life?

The first medieval mention of gold in Salzburg was in a decree of Louis the Pious in 908. In it the Emperor awarded to the canon the royal villa of Salzburghofen and the right to the salt and gold found in the diocese. From then on, from time to time, mention was made of the bishop's right to this precious metal. Until the fourteenth century the placer miners washed out the gold from the sands of the mountain streams until they reached the source of the ore. Thereafter, only persons experienced in the art of mining were able to engage in the business. The first documentary of Salzburg's gold mining operation and a method for financing it was issued by Archbishop Rudolph in May, 1287, and in one of 1292 Konrad of Salzburg spoke of gold mining in the Pinzgau.

At approximately the beginning of the fourteenth century, the industry had reached its peak of production through a system of capitalistic enterprise stimulated by the ever mounting need for funds to finance the ambitious enterprise of the prince-archbishop. His agents carefully supervised the operations to assure to him the maximum return. A ten percent severance tax was collected, of which the owner of the mining land and the superintendent each received one-tenth. The ore had to be crushed and ground in the machines of the prelate and refined in his furnaces. It was he who determined the fineness of the metal for its coinage. A native of Florence, the first city of Italy to adopt its own system of coinage, was the first master of the Salzburg mint.

Commerce between Salzburg and Italian cities had reached a fairly high state of development at the beginning of the thirteenth century. Profitable trade relations then existed between merchants of Venice and of the city of Salzburg and other towns in the archbishopric. Merchants privileged to engage in the Venetian trade proudly displayed its coat of arms, the head of a lion holding a ring in its mouth. Emperor Frederick III, in 1480, authorized merchants of Salzburg to transport Venetian wares by way of the Salzach, the Inn, and the Danube to Vienna. Italian artisans, gold and silver smiths, painters, wood carvers, sculptors, and stone masons traveled along this road to Salzburg to participate in construction work and the beautification of the seat of the archbishopric.

The original castle, *Festung* (fortress) Hohensalzburg, was erected (1066-1088) by Archbishop Gebhard and enlarged by his successors. In its "Golden Room" are the huge stove of colored glazed tile, dating from 1501, and the famous "Salzburg Stier" (bull), a mechanical organ originally of all wood pipes built in 1502, so called because of its deep bull-like tones when played. The Romanesque nave of the *Franziskanerkirche* (Franciscan church) was built in the thirteenth century and the parish church was built in 1408. The foundation of the *Stiftkirche St. Peter* (Abbey Church) was laid in 846, and the Romanesque church, which was frequently altered, was built in 1127. A few steps from the church is the famous *Peterskeller* (Peter's Cellar) hewn out of the rock of the *Moenchsberg,* the most popular restaurant of Salzburg, noted for its *Stiftsplatte* (Abbey Platter for two). To the left of the Stiftskeller is the old cemetery dominated by the fortress. Centered in the churchyard is the St. Margret's Chapel (1491) and at the slope of the mountain is the Chapel of the Holy Cross (1170). The staircase from here hewn out of solid rock leads up to the catacombs. The *Rathaus* (Town Hall) was built in 1407 and completely rebuilt in 1775. One of Salzburg's oldest churches is the Augustinerkirche, first spoken of in authentic records in 1148; it was rebuilt in 1453.

In the course of the fourteenth and fifteenth centuries the city of Salzburg evolved into a busy and prosperous community. The commercial and mining enterprises of the principality then experienced a marked expansion. New lands were made available and cleared for cultivation. The elaborate household maintained by the prince-archbishop, the palatial structures built by him, the town houses constructed by the nobles, as well as the business activity of an industrious burgher class did much to make Salzburg one of the beautiful towns of Europe. The castle Neuhausen, built by Archbishop Eberhard III (d. 1428) for a summer residence overlooking the village of Guil, afforded him a panoramic view of the picturesque, verdant valley of the Salzach.

Little has been done since the early Middle Ages to improve the means of communication in the archbishopric. No overland roads in a real sense were maintained. Vehicular transportation was possible only over the plain, and travel through the uplands proceeded along narrow mountain trails. The main route north was by way of the hamlet Wagin to the Abz River, thence to Mueldorf, where it crossed a bridge over the Inn River and along it to Regensburg on the Danube.

The outward splendor and the prosperity of the city profited the peasants nothing. Their status had progressively worsened after emancipation from serfdom. The transition from a land economy to a money economy bore heavily on the freed peasant. He was obliged to pay a tax on all property improvements, a kitchen tax, a government tax, and the tithe, an annual money payment for the support of the church. Beginning in the second half of the fourteenth century, a fee called *Weihsteuer* was collected from him to assist in defraying the papal charge for the consecration of a newly chosen archbishop and the bestowal of the pallium upon him. Other assessments were levied against him, such as payment to defray the expense for military service, a tax of one-fiftieth of the sale value of any property sold, as well as a recording fee. Through payments in kind the cathedral chapter obtained at one time 505 horses and large quantities of cheese from dairying communities. Irksome services, like cutting firewood for his former lord, work on roads, and similar obligations that had been inherited from the age of serfdom, were still demanded of him.

48

From sources other than taxes Archbishops Ortolf and Pilgrim II had an annual income of 30,000 Goldgulden,[1] but neither was able to get along on this. Pilgrim II secured loans from a Prior Hans von Zinzendorf, a burgher Niklas Teisinger, two Jews named Marchlin and Kaschinn, and from bankers of Florence, Siena and Rome. In return for the support of the duke of Bavaria for his elevation to office, Pilgrim II paid 16,000 Gulden. His vassals demanded money payment for military services, and other expenses were in the amount of 5,280 Gulden. Papal subsidies between 1313 and 1377 were in the total amount of 6,600 Gulden. The expense for a biennial attendance at the court of the pope was considerable.

The inflationary trends and the added burden of taxes for the support of the hierarchical expenses of Salzburg made the oppressed peasant sullen and resentful. Nothing was done to lighten his burdens, and the plea for relief from the flooding of his land with stagnant waters from the mining operations at the Duerrnberg was ignored. Peasants of Pongau, Pinzgau, and Bixenthal, who staged an unsuccessful revolt in 1462, demanded a well-ordered system of justice, a fixed rate of taxation, and a limit set for clerical financial demands. Feuds that also arose between burghers and craftsmen, who resented rights enjoyed by burghers, were such as to call for police intervention.

Following years of economic distress, the Salzburg knights organized the so-called *Ingelbund* in May, 1403. It criticized the extravagance of the archbishop and raised its voice against the steady flow of money to Rome without the knowledge of the various classes in the diocese. It decried the burden of debt saddled on the community, the customary practice of levying extraordinary taxes, and it condemned the practice of appointing and consecrating an archbishop without popular approval. The practice of imprisonment for minor debts, which had as its exclusive purpose the collection of heavy fines for revenue, was most obnoxious to the Salzburg knights. The practice of requiring widows and orphans to be wed without the approval of their relatives was decried by the Bund. The Bund issued a manifesto calling on the archbishop to respect old customs affecting knights, servants, guildsmen, and all others, whether rich or poor. In the future, his recognition or that of his

----

[1] A gulden of 1527 had a purchasing power of about ten dollars in American money in 1930. Its purchasing power must have been considerably more in the fourteenth century.

successors by the *Bund* would be granted only after its demands had been honored. Should he impose unwarranted burdens on anyone, he would be called to account and, in case he failed to make amends, the matter would be referred to the *Kammergericht,* the Imperial Court.

The provost of the cathedral chapter, Eberhard III (1403-1427) of Neuhaus, was elected archbishop three days after the manifesto was announced. No sooner had he assumed the duties of his office than he granted relief from certain financial exactions. His decree had hardly been proclaimed, when the Jewish creditors to his predecessor were haled into court; here they were charged with usurious practices, convicted, fined, and had their property confiscated.[2] He knew full well that his action would have the approval of the public and particularly of those indebted to persons of a despised and persecuted race. Until May, 1403, Jewish and Christian relations had been quite amicable in Salzburg. But, on July 10, Eberhard III announced that reports of Jewish persecutions and the burning of their homes had come to his attention. At Hallein Jewish homes were put to the torch with the exception of those of a wealthy Jew, two Jewish women who embraced the Christian faith, and Jewish children. The pretext for such dastardly acts was the claim that the victims had entered Christian sanctuaries and had desecrated the consecrated host by removing it from the monstrance. It would seem that on some such pretext Eberhard justified the confiscation of those Jewish homes which he awarded to his two brothers.

Such criminal subterfuge failed to meet Eberhard's financial needs. For he soon found it necessary to negotiate liens wherever willing creditors could be found or pressured. The financial stringency of the episcopy was heightened by the refusal of the Pope to approve the appointment of Eberhard. Instead, at the urgent request of the Austrian archduke, one named Berchtold was appointed. To win popular acclaim, the new appointee announced a reduction of taxes and then turned to the Medici of Florence for a loan. When the cathedral chapter refused to confirm the appointment of Berchtold, Eberhard assumed the office and the Pope de-

---

[2]This was a common practice in the Middle Ages. Princes would borrow from Jewish moneylenders, permit them to collect interest, prohibited under medieval law, and in case of financial distress would proceed against them.

manded that he pay Berchtold's loan due the Medici as well as an annual pension of 2,000 florins.

To the resentment against an increase in the cost of religious services held as a monopoly by the churchmen must be added the decline in respect for the clergy because of their moral depravity. A general decline of discipline within the rank and file of the clergy was proportionate to the confused state of Christendom for more than a century. This state of confusion emerged out of the violent and uncompromising conflict between Philip IV of France and Pope Boniface VIII. When Boniface died in 1303, Philip had a Frenchman, who chose the name Clement V, elevated to the papal office. Influenced by the French king and fearful of the factional turmoil in Rome, Clement established his residence in the city of Avignon in France in 1308. Though technically independent of France and a fief of the Holy Roman Empire, a pope who resided at Avignon could hardly expect to escape the influence of the French court. The residence of the Pope at Avignon from 1309 to 1378 was called the "Babylon Captivity" of the papacy. Unfortunately this era was followed by the "Great Schism," a period in which Christendom was forced to choose between two and finally three popes. The papacy, and with it much of the clergy, had been so scandalized that Emperor Sigismund had a church council meet at Constance, in 1414, to remedy this evil. Even the best of the pontiffs was helpless to combat the cancerous evils of the time. Sadly enough, most of the popes of the fourteenth and fifteenth centuries were believed by contemporaries to be willing to stoop to any form of vice or crime.

The higher clerical offices in Salzburg, as in the rest of Germany, were regarded as prizes to be held by members of the high ranking nobility. All too often, younger nobles of high rank, without any clerical training or experience, were consecrated as bishops or archbishops. Contrary to canon law, these officials delayed taking holy orders as long as possible; and some, after having taken title to coveted lands belonging to the patrimony of the church, returned to the status of laymen. Every one of the prelates of Salzburg in the fourteenth and fifteenth centuries was a layman. Some, without papal challenge, proclaimed themselves Legates of the Apostolic See and went so far as to issue decrees as papal nuncios, and professed to speak by virtue of papal authority.

51

In 1368, a chronicler of Salzburg accused the clerks, priests of churches and chapels, and rectors of schools of disobeying their spiritual advisers, and of refusing to assist in dispensing the sacraments and to visit parishioners. He further charged that churches had been made into places of business where priests were telling fortunes by observing the position of certain stars, the moon, and the constellations. In 1311, a pastor was removed from office for murder, and Archbishop Frederick III ordered the removal of a priest for seducing a nun. In 1377, another was charged with a similar act involving a girl aged thirteen. These were not isolated cases, for many other accusations were made against the priesthood: such as murder, bearing arms, absenting themselves from official functions and failing to wear their ministerial garb, frequenting taverns, engaging in dice games, keeping concubines, failing to surrender papal dues collected by them, neglecting to pay their debts, and committing acts of perjury. The evils most difficult to curb were those of concubinage and illegitimacy, which were current ever since celibacy had been made mandatory for the clergy.

Fortunately at a time when the church seemed to have reached an all-time low, new spiritual forces from within and others from without emerged to rectify an intolerable situation. As respect for the secular clergy waned, and devout Christians began to doubt the efficacy of sacraments administered by a decadent priesthood, the regular clergy, those living by monastic rules, were available for spiritual guidance. Such were the mendicant friars of the order of St. Francis and St. Dominic in the thirteenth century and those of St. Augustine of the fourteenth century. These were dedicated to a rigid adherence to the Benedictine rule of poverty, chastity, and obedience. Through an exemplary life and spiritual sincerity, they in time did much to raise the moral and intellectual standards of the priesthood.

CHAPTER VII

THE AGE OF THE REFORMATION

THE PRINCE-ARCHBISHOPRIC of Salzburg, beset by a declining economy and a decadent clergy in the sixteenth century, could hardly expect to escape the intellectual and religious challenges which harassed the Roman Church in the sixteenth and seventeenth centuries. Neither the Franciscan and Dominican orders, born in an atmosphere of spiritual decline and secular enlightenment, nor the crusading efforts of the church were able to prevail. Whether the teachings of Peter Waldo, who in 1173 renounced his wealth and founded the lay order of the Poor Men of Lyons and preached in the vernacular, ever reached Salzburg is highly questionable. The Waldensian heresy did, however, penetrate into the Rhineland and the nearby states of Swabia and Bohemia. Without a doubt the doctrines of John Huss, for which he was condemned by the Council of Constance and burned at the stake in 1414, did find acceptance in Salzburg.

Archbishop Eberhard III, at a province council in 1420, declared that the heretical teachings of the Wycliffites and Hussites had crept in as a wolf in sheep's clothing, and that their converts had the audacity to teach and defend the heresies. He zealously sought to enforce the Conciliar decree which ordered the extirpation of the doctrines of Huss, professor at the University of Prague in Bohemia. In spite of the archbishop's efforts, it is believed that the embers of the new doctrine continued to smolder in remote and isolated agricultural and mining communities until the time of Luther one hundred years later. It is an established fact that the seed of Lutheranism found almost immediate root in the same areas. Cardinal Bellarmenus frankly admitted the spread of the so-called "Lutheran Pest" "like wildfire," and declared, "The doctrine which originated in Saxony had enflamed all of Germany and thence had spread to the Scandinavian countries, France, England, Scotland, the Alpine states including Salzburg and even Italy."

In the first two decades of the spread of the "Lutheran Pest" Matthew Lang, archbishop of Salzburg (1519-1540), was an advisor to Emperor Charles V. He was born in 1467 in Augsburg of impoverished patrician parentage. Thirty years later, after he had attained prominence in the councils of the Empire, the family was ennobled. He was educated in the humanistic atmosphere of the universities of Tuebingen and Ingolstadt, which were dedicated to the liberal arts, theology and jurisprudence, where he specialized in theology and jurisprudence. At the University of Vienna, where he matriculated in 1493, his scholarly attainments brought him an appointment to the staff of the Austrian Chancery. In 1494 we find him a confidential adviser to Maximilian I, Emperor of the Holy Roman Empire, and soon thereafter he was appointed his private secretary. In that capacity he was entrusted with most difficult diplomatic assignments.

Matthew Lang was the product of a generation when the cultural trends of the past seem to have been woven into a pattern which gave birth to one of the great epochs of history, the Reformation. Rarely in the history of man has such a galaxy of outstanding personalities appeared in so short a time on the human stage in the field of politics, religion, economics, arts and science.

This confidant of Maximilian was, first of all, a man of the world. By 1506 his income from holdings and gifts from the Emperor and bribes, a practice then common in the field of diplomacy, amounted to 60,000 gulden. He was a lover of splendor and showmanship, and on special occasions he was wont to put on an appearance which set him off in striking contrast to others of like rank. He was a connoisseur of art and a patron of literature. In no sense of the word was he a churchman, and he enjoyed reveling in sumptuous banquets, gay affairs, and dances, and was a lion with members of the fair sex. A contemporary said that few persons of note in all of Germany could match the covetous and inflated ambitious desire of this obstinate son of an Augsburg burgher. Rem, a chronicler at Augsburg, called him a "Schuerzenjaeger," (apron or petticoat chaser) whose capers at Halloween celebrations could hardly be described in polite society.

In recognition for his part in establishing amicable relations between Pope Leo X and the German Emperor, Lang was tendered the cap of a cardinal and admitted to membership in the college. By no means did this suffice, for, at the death of Archbishop

Leonard of Salzburg, June 8, 1519, he demanded and was elevated to the post of the latter. On September 23, he made his triumphal entry into Salzburg, there to be consecrated as priest and bishop and formally cloaked with the pallium. To all who attended the first Mass celebrated by Lang was promised a special papal indulgence.

None of his predecessors ever matched his brazen and insatiable nepotism. The Lang family was housed in the residence of the chief of the cathedral chapter. Its members received large land grants, and the income from these was augmented by liberal money payments from Matthew. Though the major part of the lands of the archbishopric were parceled out to members of his family, he nevertheless, if not the richest prince, was reckoned one of the richest of his day.

The major part of the archbishop's income was derived from the salt produced at the salt works of Hallein and the mining of precious metals at Tauern. By 1506 the production and sale of salt was monopolized by Lang. No less important to him were other mining operations, which had reached a high stage of production through domestic and foreign capitalist enterprise. In 1460 the mining industry was able to boast of thirty different operational centers. About 20,000 workers were employed in 1,000 gold and silver mining pits. One in the Krone mine yielded an income of 80,000 ducats. The estimated annual value of mining operations was 977,280 Gulden. The total monetary value of gold and silver mined between 1460 and 1550 was about 7,729,696 Gulden. The entrepreneur's chief concern was immediate gain regardless of its effect on the future. In time the oversupply of gold and silver derived from these operations and the influx of those metals from the Americas created an inflationary and economic crisis throughout Europe. The peasants and mountain folk were most seriously affected and their desperate plight was a contributing factor in the peasant revolts of the first half of the sixteenth century.

Lang's stay in Salzburg was cut short by important matters affecting the Empire. Charles, the grandson of Maximilian I and of Ferdinand and Isabella, who had succeeded to the throne of Spain (1516) as Carlos I and to that of the grandfather (1519) as Charles V, summoned Lang to Spain as his adviser. With Charles he attended the Diet of Worms (1521) before which Martin Luther was to appear and answer regarding his "heretical" teachings. Lang had a part in maneuvering the trial of Luther and in formulating the Edict of Worms which outlawed him after he had reaffirmed his teachings in the presence of Charles V and the Imperial Diet.

Nine years later Lang was present at the Diet of Augsburg, where Charles V refused to recognize the Augsburg Confession, which was formulated and presented to the Diet by the scholar Melanchthon, and threatened to suppress the Lutheran heresy by force of arms. In protest the followers of Luther met a year later at Schmalkald to organize a league to defend their rights as granted at the Diet of Speyer (1526), which declared that "Each prince should conduct himself so he could answer for his behavior to God and to the emperor." Lang, who had a part in forming the first Catholic League and the later and stronger one at Nuernberg (1538), was instrumental in inducing the Duke of Bavaria, a hereditary enemy of the Austrian Hapsburgs, to withdraw from the League of Schmalkald when the tide of events was turning in favor of the Emperor and thus endangering the prestige and the spiritual primacy of the Pope.

Martin Luther had hardly made public his 95 theses against indulgences, October 31, 1517, when repercussions of his statements were heard in Salzburg. Later, both Stephan Agricola and Paul Speratus ventured to preach Luther's new doctrine from the pulpit of the Salzburg cathedral. Speratus found it necessary to flee from Salzburg and find refuge in Olmuetz and later in Wittenberg. Later he was appointed archbishop of the Evangelical church of Pomerania by Albrecht, Elector of Brandenburg. His German translation of Luther's Latin text of *On the Selection and Training of a Pastor* was dedicated to the Lutherans of Salzburg. In it he called on them to hold to their faith secretly should they be unable to do so publicly.

Agricola was brought to trial and ordered to the dungeon of a tower in the city wall where barrels of powder had been stored. It was said that a plot was carefully laid to have the powder exploded immediately after his incarceration, to be followed by a public announcement that fire from heaven had ignited the powder to destroy the heretic. His late arrival, however, and a premature explosion caused the plot to miscarry. Amid the confusion which followed, he was released from chains and permitted to escape, and his compatriots could now claim for him a providential deliverance.

George Schaerer, a Franciscan in the Tefsereg Valley near the Swiss border, renounced his novitiate, cast aside his official frock, and publicly proclaimed Luther's doctrine at Radstadt. For this he was arrested, convicted, and executed for violating his oath. Other defections from the Catholic faith were then quite common, and, in the course of time, stories of martyrdom and accounts of miraculous deliverance found their way into the Lutheran folk lore.

Was it perhaps to meet the demands for clerical reform and greater emphasis on preaching at the level of the common man or was it to disassociate Johann von Staupitz[1] from his student and friend, Martin Luther, that Matthew Lang invited the former to Salzburg in 1520? Lang may have been impressed by the preaching of von Staupitz, his mild manner, and his demand for an inward reform of man and of the church. Von Staupitz, like his protégé, Luther, stressed justification by faith rather than good works.

The execution of Luther's supporters ordered by Archbishop Matthew Lang, and perhaps Luther's tract, *The Freedom of the Common Man,* helped to inflame many of the peasants and miners and were in a measure immediately responsible for the invasion of the city of Salzburg by the peasants and mine workers of the principality who were also faced with heavier taxes and political restrictions. The revolt begun by them was crushed and its leaders were punished. A forced loan of 4,000 Gulden levied against the burghers and the city charter, as revised by Lang, all but wiped out their privileges. A military reserve was created, the fortresses around the city were re-enforced, and their guns were so mounted as to guard against subsequent insurrections. But nothing was done to remedy the underlying causes of discontent. In Pongau and Pinzgau unredeemed promises made to end a peasant revolt in 1462 contributed to violence there. All of this and the gearing of justice to revenue in Salzburg as well as in other German church principalities and the increased financial exactions made these the center

---

[1]Staupitz was the father superior of the Augustinian Order to which Luther belonged and professor of theology at the University of Wittenberg. In 1511 he requested Luther's appointment to the staff of the University of Wittenberg. The following year, after Luther had been awarded the title Dr. of Theology, von Staupitz relinquished his professorate to his former student and friend, an office which Luther held until his death. Staupitz and the Elector of Saxony supported Luther's refusal to recant his doctrines after his trial before the Diet of Worms (1519).

of origin of the Peasants' War in 1525, from which it was spread to the rest of Germany.

Unable to stem the tide of Lutheranism in northern Germany after 1524, the papal legate to Germany summoned all spiritual as well as temporal princes to a conference at Regensburg. Here the princes of Bavaria, Austria, Salzburg and the Bishop of Strassburg agreed to support each other in the enforcement of the Edict of Worms (1521), which condemned and outlawed Luther and ordered the surrender and confiscation of all Lutheran literature. All subjects of the princes concerned were to be prohibited from attending the University of Wittenberg.

The immediate cause of the Peasants' War in Salzburg was the arrest of a priest for teaching Lutheran doctrines. On his way to prison through Schellenberg his guards were attacked by ruffians who released the prisoner. The peasants, who were enraged by the executions of their fellows without a hearing, rebelled. The mountaineers were called to action by the sound of drums and signal fires. They forced their way through the city gate, pillaged the town houses of the nobles and forced Lang, his household, the cathedral chapter, and the bishop's retainers to take refuge in the castle Hohensalzburg. For twelve weeks the castle was besieged. Not until Ludwig of Bavaria had moved in his forces and the peasants had been promised amnesty was the siege lifted.

Once the revolutionists had withdrawn, the promise of amnesty was ignored, and vengeance was inflicted upon the areas where trouble had originated. Radstadt, the center of the movement, was forced to bear the brunt of the punishment. On July 11, 1526, its population, upon pain of death, was forced to take an oath of allegiance to the prince, surrender all arms, return what had been stolen, and pay a fine of 14,000 Gulden to compensate for loss by fire. Twenty-seven of the town's leaders were summarily beheaded. An indemnity of 100,000 Gulden was charged against its citizens to be paid in five annual installments in partial payment of the 300,000 Gulden expended for supressing the revolt. The loss of cattle and the resultant shortage of meat made necessary meat imports from Austria. In consequence of the siege of Hohensalzburg the archbishop was obliged to content himself with one trumpeter. In April, 1528, his need for horses was so acute that he found it necessary to compel each of four of his monastic orders to loan him one manservant and two horses. On an occasion when he discovered a plot to make Salzburg a free, imperial city, he ordered twenty of its leaders executed.

There was, perhaps, less outside or foreign cultural influence to be found in Salzburg than in any other German principality at that time. The only exceptions were for Italian art, Spanish or French etiquette, and homage to the Roman See. In his capacity of papal legate the word of the Archbishop of Salzburg was final in most controversial matters and therefore need not be submitted to the Pope. Should the chair of bishop in the bishopric on the Chiemsee be vacated in a specified month, Archbishop Matthew Lang was privileged to appoint a successor without papal authorization. In his administration the Archbishop of Salzburg was called *Primus Germanicus* (Primate of Germany). Lang ranked first in the assembly of the lords spiritual of the German Reichstag. He, unlike the prince-bishops of Mainz, Fulda, Wuerzburg, Kempen, Gronenbach, and Herbishofen, refused publicly to compromise with Protestantism.

In dealing with the religious question in his diocese, Lang was less successful. He seemed to want to do something about it, but lacked a consistent determination to come to grips with it. Perhaps the effect of concerted action posed too great a threat to the economy of the arch-bishopric, since the discontent was centered in the mining communities. Furthermore, the necessary agencies for coming to grips with Protestantism were not at hand and his broader interest in clerical reform and international diplomacy left him little time to concentrate on affairs of Salzburg. In the city itself and the market centers the populace had suffered sufficient public intimidation to compel their religious conformity. The urban as well as the rural population was not resentful of the Church as such, but was motivated by a fervent spiritual desire for a fundamental change in the church service. They demanded the use of the German language in such things as the Mass, spiritual songs, liturgy, and the sacraments, with a pastor of their own choice.

Lang's successor Ernst (1540-1554) was the son of the Archduke of Bavaria and of the daughter of Maximilian I. He showed little interest in clerical affairs for which he had been educated. His associates, who wished to have him vested with the rank of a cardinal, urged that there be no let-up in combating Protestantism and in loyalty to Rome. The Pope, who was well aware of

Ernst's lack of interest in matters spiritual, refused to make the coveted appointment.

Ernst did nothing to keep pace with the trend toward founding humanist institutions of higher learning and did little to raise the moral and intellectual level of his clergy. Complaints were current that priests absented themselves from auricular confession, served both bread and wine to communicants, disregarded fasts, and did nothing to prevent the reading of heretical books and Protestant clergy from entering the principality of Salzburg. In 1553, Ernst's order that priests refuse the sacrament to all who insisted upon partaking of the wine was generally ignored.

In 1550, a coadjutor was appointed for Ernst, but four years later, having failed to be consecrated to the office, he resigned. A new coadjutor, Michael, was then appointed to hold office until 1560. He was deeply concerned with needed clerical reforms and showed an abiding interest in orthodox Catholicism. When the Archduke of Bavaria proclaimed that no one was to be punished for refusing the Sacrament when denied the cup, or for eating meat on fast days, Michael remarked: "Even Bavaria has departed from the Catholic faith." Like his predecessors, he found that orders against concubinage of the priesthood were ignored. Even among the rank and file of the cathedral chapter, celibacy was the exception rather than the rule.

CHAPTER VIII

FROM THE CATHOLIC REFORMATION TO 1648

ON THE pretext of an abiding concern for the threat of heretics to the peace of Salzburg neither Ernst nor Michael bothered particularly about the deliberations of the Council of Trent.[1] For the same reason Archbishop John-Jacob von Kuen (1560-1586), a man of deep spiritual and moral conviction, declined to attend, but sent personal representatives to request a modification of the church's stand on the denial of the cup to laymen in Holy Communion. Failing to gain recognition and a vote in the council, two of the three delegates departed in disgust. In the end the practice of permitting the communicant to partake of the wine was terminated, in 1565.

The enforcement of the Conciliar decree by John-Jacob incited a revolt in the mountain communities where the privilege of permitting communicants to use the wine had been enjoyed for some years. On January 18, 1556, Spangenberg, a priest, called upon all devout Christians of Salzburg to go to Austria to partake of the Sacrament in case the chalice was denied them. A parish priest several times expelled for his heretical sermons had been appointed to head the church of St. Veit by the peasants of Pongau in 1564. Throughout the winter of that year rebellious bands roamed the countryside and met from time to time. Peasants had been told that a certain bell-signal and discharge of muskets would summon them for meetings to be held at designated places. To cope with the mountain disturbances, mercenaries were engaged and quartered at Radstadt and the castle at Werfen,

[1] The Council of Trent was called (1545-1563) to carry out the resolutions of the Council of Constance (1414-1418) which demanded a clarification of the doctrines of the Catholic church and a reform in abuses which had scandalized all of Christendom. Owing to a disagreement over the matter of sovereignty within the church, action was postponed until after Protestantism had been widely accepted. Not until the primacy of the Pope had been established through the efforts of the Jesuits did the Council of Trent conclude its work.

where the uprisings were concentrated. To prevent interference with arrest in outlying communities heretical leaders were apprehended secretly and whisked off to be imprisoned in the fortress at Salzburg, where the sight of soldiers discouraged violence.

In response to an order from the Prince of Salzburg, an assembly representing four estates, clergy, nobility, burghers, and peasants levied the cost for military action against the community involved. It further decreed that any person guilty of violating Bishop John-Jacob's order was punishable with the loss of life or limb, and that anyone leaving the country without permission was to have his property confiscated. Attendance of Mass and Confession was made a prerequisite to partaking of Holy Communion. Baptism, if performed in the vernacular, had to follow the form agreed upon at a church council in 1557. German singing in religious services and the matter of eating meat on fast days was specially proscribed. All copies of books, songs, hymns printed or written, and religious pictures had to be delivered to a censor within eight days to be sorted, and those spiritually inoffensive were to be returned to their former owners. A variety of other religious restrictions were laid down and rigidly enforced. The previous concession on the sacraments, granted to calm peasant disturbances, was withdrawn March 15, 1571, and all heretical books found in the capital were to be confiscated. Anyone refusing the Holy Supper as ordered was to be banished or, should he be at the point of death, he should be denied burial in consecrated ground.

In the seven years which intervened between John-Jacob's stroke and his death in 1579, his coadjutor, George von Kuenburg, gave particular attention to clerical reform. He saw to it that the clerical agenda and instructions for pastoral care were revised and re-edited and he took under advisement the setting up and financing of a greatly needed theological seminary, something which was carried out by his successor.

As soon as word of John-Jacob's illness reached Salzburg's neighboring states, their rulers lost no time in promoting their candidates for the coveted office of archbishop. John-Jacob refused to be swayed by pressure from the emperor and even from the pope, and retained George as coadjutor. George, who was appointed to the episcopate, died in 1586, less than four months after his consecration as archbishop.

George's religious policy in the city of Salzburg promted the first exodus of well-to-do burghers, a movement which reached alarming proportions under his successor. If the words of a contemporary historian can be trusted, Protestantism more than held its own. "In their homes the burghers of Salzburg drink in the heretical poison from books of prayers and sermons, catechisms and hymnals. They send their sons to Lutheran *Gymnasien* outside the bishopric. A majority of the burghers, peasants in the uplands and workers in the mines are non-Catholic. It is feared all of the principality will embrace Protestantism."[2]

It was in such an atmosphere, beset with a restlessness bordering on revolt among the peasants and the mine workers, that Wolf-Dietrich von Raitenau assumed the role of prince-archbishop (1588-1612). He soon proved himself a typical Machiavellian despot. In utter disregard for the economy of Salzburg, he set out to transform the capital from a medieval to a modern city by promoting architectural splendor that would be a credit to any Renaissance potentate. At great expense he saw to the construction of palatial residences and castles for housing his brothers, sisters, relatives, and, above all, his Salome, the beautiful, even-tempered daughter of William Alt, a wealthy Salzburg merchant. When this intimate relationship began is a matter of conjecture, but it was rumored that he was so captivated by her beauty that he had her taken secretly off a ballroom floor and brought to his castle. Her residence was established close by that of Wolf-Dietrich until she and her many children by the archbishop could be settled in the Castle Altenau built for her by Wolf-Dietrich. Lavish provision was made for them and for his Salome. Wolf invested sums in amounts ranging from 4,000 to 20,000 Gulden in the wholesale business of the Steinhauers, Salzburg's wealthiest merchants. After he obtained administrative control of the treasury, Wolf made grants to Salome (1606-1611) in money, leases, houses, and land that were estimated to have amounted to 400,000 Gulden. Ten daughters and three sons of their large family were still living in 1611. Through his influence, Salome and her children were ennobled and titled von Altenau. It seemed quite apparent in the latter years of his reign that he wanted to

[2]Quoted from Arnold, C. F., *Die Vertreibung der Salzburg Protestanten* (Leipzig, 1900) p. 45.

secularize the prince-archbishopric and have it inherited by his eldest son, Hannibal von Altenau. To that end he probably omitted the episcopal emblem from his coat of arms on structures built by him; and in June, 1612, when forced to resign his office, he did so only as archbishop. The Castle Altenau and its gardens were enlarged and improved by Wolf-Dietrich's successor, Archbishop Markus Sitticus, who changed the castle's name to Myerabela (Mirabell). Entering wrought iron gates to the gardens one has a panoramic view of the fortress on the Moenchsberg, on the opposite side of the Salzach. Extensive changes were made in the palace in the second decade of the eighteenth century only to be destroyed by fire in 1818, and later rebuilt. The gorgeous garden is surrounded by a walkway flanked by shrubbery and trees. Today it is the official residence of the Lord Mayor of Salzburg with several administrative offices. The great Marble Room on the second floor is an admirable setting for chamber concerts.

In keeping with the times, a very large staff was needed to operate Wolf-Dietrich's household. Heading the personnel in 1590 was the lord high chamberlain, who also supervised the stables of his prince. In addition there were a stable master and a keeper of the silver chamber, six chamberlains, two house tailors, two butlers, six pages, four valets, two doorkeepers, six footmen, twelve lord high stewards, three foretasters and silver polishers, one personal tailor, one stoker and sweeper, one master of the cellar and two helpers, one binder, two master and two chief cooks, three kitchen lads for the nobles, two chief cooks and three kitchen boys for the servants, and one master of the household who supervised matters of immediate concern to the mansion. Added in 1599 were two noblemen and marshal of the court, two court chaplains, an instructor for pages, a master of the chase, sixteen court musicians — three of them Italians, eight trumpeters and a drummer, a court jeweler, a Dutch embroiderer, a personal barber, a bather, a tailor, and a shoemaker. Other personnel indirectly concerned were members of the court council, body guards, castle garrison and servants, court architect, city administrator and night-watchmen, in all about 286 persons. Unfortunately, no record is extant of the amount of wine consumed, which must have been very large, as the prince-archbishop was a lavish entertainer. He was also wont to shower his guests with expensive gifts.

His liberal almsgiving necessitated his having to lay down rules regulating the practice of begging. In 1608, workers and children were prohibited from requesting alms at court or of the bishop on the street. All impoverished persons were ordered to be sent from the city. Should they return they should be put in chains for a day at hard labor with a slice of bread. Wolf-Dietrich was especially liberal at almsgiving on All Souls Day. A chronicler in 1608 reported that in November he gave to 1600 persons.

In addition to the expense of his elaborate household, the regular assessments for the imperial and district governments and the league of the mountain states were considerable. Year after year the archbishop sent 500 men to Hungary to help hold back a Turk invasion. The cost of these expeditions and similar actions in 1599 amounted to approximately 600,000 Gulden.

In the interim preceding Wolf-Dietrich's election as archbishop by the cathedral chapter, Austria had groomed a scion of the House of Hapsburg, while Bavaria had favored a member of the Augsburg house of Fugger, the wealthiest in Germany. However, the ultimate and unexpected choice of Wolf-Dietrich as archbishop soon found favor with the Pope and with the Bavarian archduke. In no manner committed to the Salzburg tradition, Wolf-Dietrich was able to aprroach more objectively than his predecessors the economic, political, and religious problems of the prince-archbishopric. To that end he had gained, through extensive travel and association, an intimate understanding of people. Had it not been for his arrogance and his opinionated self-importance, he might have been a more successful administrator.

One of his first acts as prince-archbishop was to come to grips with the Anabaptists and Lutherans. He should like to have called upon the Jesuits, an order born in the atmosphere of the Catholic Counter-Reformation, to rid Salzburg of these "heretical pests." While urging William of Bavaria to employ the Jesuits for a similar purpose, he frankly admitted that to do so for Salzburg might have serious consequences. Upon his return from Rome, where he had been well received, Wolf demanded either an oath of allegiance to Catholicism or the resignation of non-juring government officials. Each was instructed to be on constant guard for nonconformists and to make every effort to lead them back to the

Catholic fold. Any person who refused to return to the faith of the fathers was to be banished. Upon three days' notice he was to be deprived of citizenship and sent over the border if he failed to repent. His property could be sold or leased only to a Catholic. No house was to be left without an occupant or closed to official visitors.

Large numbers of the more prosperous and enterprising burghers migrated from the capital to find refuge in Augsburg, Nuernberg, Ratisbon, and other German cities. Protestant princes who condemned Wolf's action interceded for the banished Salzburgers at the Reichstag in Ratisbon. In response, Emperor Rudolph II, who was pursuing a somewhat similar policy for reasons of expediency, sent a representative to intercede. Needless to say, all efforts toward a more considerate policy came to naught. Capuchin monks of the Franciscan order were brought in and settled in the mountain communities, in the hope that their folksy sermons might counteract the popular apeal of Lutheranism. Wolf-Dietrich dispatched Benedictines into Werfen to give instruction in the Catholic faith, and to win support through persuasion rather than force. As they proceeded in their house-to-house canvass and instruction, they encountered many who had departed from the Catholic faith.

His decrees give some idea of his interest in education and health. In his ordinance of education for Salzburg of 1593 he severely criticized the tactics of the teachers of his day. In it they were ordered to desist from the use of unusual phrases and profane words when reprimanding students. In cases of chastisement they were to spare the head and other vital members of the child's body. Though he did not oppose the use of the rod, he believed the schoolmaster's policy should be governed by a desire to instill in the student love rather than resentment. Wolf-Dietrich was far ahead of his time when he ordered the construction of an isolation barrack for the quarantine of plague victims.

Was Wolf-Dietrich's policy of moderation in the uplands adopted because he feared that an upheaval might cripple a mining industry already in a state of economic decline? Certainly a loss of employees in the salt works would have been detrimental to his chief source of income. Was it, perhaps, to placate the non-Catholic princes and obtain their tacit approval for a secularization of the prince-archbishopric? In 1609, but a few years before his flight from Salzburg, he was known to have remarked that one's conscience should guide him in matters spiritual and that he counted many evangelicals among his loyal subjects. At about the same time he adopted a more independent attitude toward Rome. His policy, however, failed to calm a freedom-loving mountain people faced with an increase in payment for the "Bread of Life" and the extravagances of Wolf. To guard against possible violence and from poaching on Wolf's hunting preserve, peasants were forbidden to carry arms; and to threaten anyone with knife or sword was made punishable by death. Drunkenness and vice were likewise condemned.

Wolf was far more successful in transforming Salzburg into a political dictatorship than he was in wiping out Protestantism. He deprived the Cathedral chapter of its authority to appoint important diocesan officials, and he ceased to submit to the chapter matters of vital concern. Rights of the burghers were all but destroyed by Wolf's refusal to call a meeting of the Salzburg assembly of estates.

The determination of Wolf-Dietrich to gain for himself the prestige in affairs of the German Empire once held by Lang proved his undoing. He lacked the diplomatic finesse of Lang, and his Reichstag maneuverings to place himself in a position of vantage vis-à-vis the emperor in war against the Turks in Hun-war with Bavaria. In the debate as to whether the members of the Reich should assist the emperor in war against the Turks in Hungary, Wolf-Dietrich supported the emperor, while Maximilian I, King of Bavaria, led the opposition. On another occasion, in conjunction with the Archbishop of Cologne, the two succeeded in having themselves appear as the real champions of Catholicism to the detriment of the Bavarian. The archbishop's strategy to annex Berchtesgaden was countered by Bavaria's moving to isolate Salzburg, and the effort of Bavaria to create a cleavage between him and his Catholic subjects.

The cold war reached a climax when, in violation of a treaty between Salzburg and Bavaria, Wolf-Dietrich raised the price of export salt to Bavaria without the approval of its ruler. In part, the archbishop hoped to recoup his loss incurred by having to accept payment in debased Bavarian coinage. Bavaria countered by attaching all of Salzburg's revenues derived from its territorial enclaves in the duchy. The "Salt War" came to a climax when

Wolf-Dietrich boycotted the export of all salt to Bavaria, and Maximilian countered by ordering 20,000 troops to the border of Salzburg under General Tilly, later commander of the Catholic League in the Thirty Years' War. The members of the Cathedral Chapter disclaimed responsibility for what had happened. They accused Wolf-Dietrich of having failed to advise them on state matters, of being an irresponsible administrator and of conspiring with the Protestant princes against Bavaria. After re-enforcing his defenses, the archbishop, whose health had failed, lost heart and decided to flee, and to return later when the tension had ended.

In preparation for the flight seven carts were loaded with money and jewelry on the night of October 22, 1611. The next morning Salome, her Steinhauer relatives and servants set out for Flachau near Radstadt, the home of the Steinhauer iron works. On the night of the 23rd, between eight and nine o'clock, Wolf with several servants, thirteen horses, and several packwagons left for Gallin. In the meantime, Maximilian of Bavaria recieved word of the flight and proceeded to march on the city of Salzburg. On the morning of October 26, he set up residence in the palace of the archbishop, and ordered a military command of 200 foot soldiers and 100 cavalry to pursue the refugees. Wolf-Dietrich, with all his belongings, was captured on November 29. Following abusive treatment, the confiscation of all his luggage, and the removal of bandages from his feet and limbs for easing the pain suffered from swollen arteries, he was imprisoned in the castle at Salzburg where he died in 1617. On March 7, 1612, he was compelled by Maximilian of Bavaria to tender his resignation as Archbishop of Salzburg. He compelled Wolf's successor, Mark Sittich, to defray all war costs and surrender the salt export trade of the Hallein mines to Bavaria.

The Salzburg Chapter refused to appoint the Austrian candidate and appointed as archbishop Mark Sittich, who was sponsored by Bavaria and the Pope. In his short term of office, terminated by death in 1619, Sittich bent most of his energy toward weeding out Lutheranism. Here his efforts were fairly rewarding, because the Protestants were without noble leadership and without the preachers and teachers generally found in rural communities. All persons who refused to comply with his religious mandate were banished from the city. A person who returned to Catholicism had to do public penance by bearing a lighted candle on entering his parish church. All Lutheran books were ferreted out to be burned, and persons found with forbidden books were heavily fined.

Here and there, in outlying hamlets and communities, lay preachers read to the unlettered in the secrecy of their homes from Luther's German Bible and other non-Catholic literature. These folks resented the obvious worldliness of the Catholic priesthood and the Roman papacy. Concubinage and the resultant illegitimacy attributable to numerous priests and assistants were matters of common knowledge. Excessive drink and bickering within clerical ranks was all too obvious. Many churchmen were known to have converted their homes into public places for dispensing spirituous drinks. Resentment against the Latin church service and the refusal to permit a layman to drink of the wine in Holy Communion was widespread. The inquisitorial practice of the Capuchins on their pastoral rounds, their search for banned books, their insistence on attendance at mass and observance of fasts, and their distribution of blessed medallions to be worn and pictures of saints and rosaries diplayed, all tended to drive Protestantism underground.

Sittich, recognizing a crying need for clerical reform, impressed the clergy with the urgency of the situation and insisted on a faithful performance of all spiritual offices. Visitors were delegated to enter the homes of the clergy to ferret out concubines, but hardly had the inspector departed when the priest's mate returned. A Gastein judge reported that a priest named Speakher continued to live with his cook and their son, as did his assistant with his maid and their three children.

The carefully planned reform procedure of Sittich was interrupted by his unexpected death and was retarded by the events of the Thirty Years' War (1618-1648). Fortunately Salzburg was then ruled by Archbishop Paris, Count of Ladron (1619-1653), of noble south Tyrolese ancestry. No other prince of the German empire so discreetly maneuvered his ship of state as to spare it the ravages of the Thirty Years' War. Neither the Pope nor the emperor was able to alter his course. Everything in his power was done to prevent infiltration by the Catholic League and the militant Jesuit order. To maintain peace within the bounds of his state, he adopted a policy of religious moderation. Granaries were stocked against famine, fortress garrisons were strengthened,

and strategic passes were so fortified as to enable a small detachment to hold at bay an entire enemy regiment. However, when
in the last year of the war the Swedish army invaded Bavaria
(January, 1648), Archbishop Paris offered asylum to the Archduke
of Bavaria and thousands of Bavarian refugees. Only the elaborate
defenses of Salzburg and the swollen waters of the Salzach saved
the bishopric from disaster. As it was, only Mueldorf was occupied
by enemy forces.

The end of war failed to bring relief from financial exactions.
No sooner had the Archduke of Bavaria returned from exile in
Salzburg to a Bavaria faced with famine and plague than he pressed
Paris with demands for money with which to help meet the
back pay of the Bavarian army, on the pretext that it had saved
Salzburg from invasion. On January 19, 1649, Bavarian representatives pressed for immediate compliance, or Bavarian troops
would be quartered in Salzburg where an abundance of food was
still to be had. To protect the state against roving bands of pillag-
ing soldiers, Salzburg had to be kept on a war footing.

Regardless of war, Paris continued the work begun by Wolf-
Dietrich of transforming Salzburg into a modern city. In his
administration the University of Salzburg was founded. The Gymnasium was made an affiliate of the university and was liberally
endowed by its founder. At the end of war, Paris reorganized
the university and strengthened its staff by appointing to its teaching force men who had been educated at Jesuit schools. They
brought to the Salzburg University the thoroughness and efficiency
of Jesuit educational methods. When all of Germany lay prostrate.
Salzburg's Paris was publicly acclaimed the Father of his Country
and the capital city the German Rome.

CHAPTER IX

FROM WESTPHALIA[1] (1648) TO PROTESTANT EXPULSION

GUIDOBALD (1654-1668), a Bohemian nobleman and Count von Thurn, was appointed to succeed Archbishop Paris in preference to Bavaria's Prince Albrecht Siegmund, bishop of Freising, who was made bishop of Gurk at fourteen and of Trent at the age of nineteen. The new appointee was restrained neither by tradition nor by war in the pursuit of an anti-Protestant religious policy. By an order in 1655, all heretical books were to be delivered to the Salzburg consistory. Any laborer employed outside the principality must, upon his return, present an affidavit of having attended a Catholic Easter confession and partaken of Holy Communion. An oath of loyalty to the Catholic faith was made a prerequisite for readmission to citizenship, and the clergy were ordered to report all religious infractions.

The existing international crisis again gravitated against a systematic follow-through by Guidobald of Salzburg. As lord high commissioner of the Empire, much of his time had to be spent in attendance at the imperial diet in Ratisbon. Furthermore, the prince-archbishopric was obliged to meet an imperial levy of 176,000 Gulden and to furnish supplies and a contingent of soldiers for the defense of the Empire against the Turks. In addition, the troops of Louis XIV of France had to be provisioned on their march through Salzburg to join the Austrian forces. In spite of the hospitality of the Salzburgers, French criminal excesses were such as to provoke vengeance by the peasantry of Hallein, ending in the death of some of the foreign soldiers. It would seem that Louis XIV's real objective was to feel out the strength of the

---

[1]The Treaty of Westphalia recognized the principle of the territorial independence of the German princes. Calvinism was given the same legal standing as Lutheranism. Each prince or free city of Germany was authorized to enforce conformity to one of the three faiths and the expulsion of dissidents. The governments were to allow at least private worship, liberty of conscience, and the right of emigration.

Empire in anticipation of his invasion of the Spanish Netherlands in 1667. In that invasion, called the War of Devolution (1667-1668), the German diet supported the Netherlands, one of the states of the German Empire.

Protestantism in Salzburg encountered its most unyielding antagonist in Max Gandolph von Kuenburg (1668-1687), an offspring of two former prelates of Salzburg, and who now succeeded Guidobald as Archbishop of Salzburg. Steeped in the Jesuit tradition of thoroughness, educated at Gratz and at the Collegium Germanicum of Rome and being a child of an age of rabid intolerance, he was determined on nothing short of Protestant extermination, and political dictatorship. Almost immediately following consecration, he ordered church visitations in the rural upland communities, and had pastoral outposts and schools for religious education set up in sections where Catholic orthodoxy seemed to lag. Heretics, sorcerers, and witches were to be exposed publicly and tried, and Protestant "rebels" in two districts were banished. In 1685, all non-Catholics in the valley of the Teffereg, bordering on the Tyrol, were ordered out of the bishopric. Depending upon circumstances, they were given from fourteen days to eight weeks to leave. Children under fifteen were not allowed to leave, "in order that their souls might be saved through Catholic indoctrination". In most instances, persons banished were not given time to dispose of their property. Some who attempted to take their children were taken into custody and thrown into an underground dungeon in the Salzburg fortress. Their property was confiscated, and their children were committed to monasteries.

Many of the emigrants found refuge in Ratisbon, where they filed protests with the conclave of Protestant princes. Others found refuge in Nuernburg, Augsburg, Ulm, and Leipzig. In these cities Protestant pastors supplied them with religious literature to be smuggled into Salzburg. Samuel Urlsperger, Evangelical minister of Augsburg and pastor of St. Anne's church, looked after the needs of the Salzburg refugees and assisted apprentices in finding employment. It was he who, at a later date as a trustee of the British colony of Georgia, saw to the settlement of Salzburgers in that colony.

Max Gandolph's first positive action against Lutheranism in the mining regions was the arrest of three of their leaders. Two of those arrested, who failed to recant in the allotted two weeks, were the Scheitberger brothers, Samuel and Joseph. The younger, Joseph, was so outspoken in his defense of Lutheranism that he was lodged in prison, where two Capuchin monks undertook to convert him. This having failed, he was taken to the frontier for deportation. Through secret parental instruction in the Bible and a comparison of the Lutheran and Catholic catechism with Holy Writ Joseph's Lutheran convictions were confirmed. To counteract any charge which might have been made by the Protestant princes at the Ratisbon Diet that the method of the banishment of Lutherans was contrary to the provisions of the Treaty of Westphalia, Gandolph had the expulsion charge made to read a "forbidden doctrine."

Persons apprehended in an attempted escape were put in irons, and those who refused to recant were set across the border. Their children were held to be reared in the Catholic faith, the parental property was confiscated and supposedly applied toward the children's support. It was not unusual for parents to return secretly to see their children and abduct them if possible. The loyal Catholic children of Joseph Scheitberger refused to follow him when he secretly returned to abduct them. When Protestant princes interceded on behalf of the children and protested against arbitrary confiscation of property, they were told that the children refused to leave and that the property confiscated was inadequate to their support.

For over a half century Joseph Scheitberger was a thorn in the flesh of the Salzburg theocracy. From Nuernberg, where he engaged in a profitable business, Joseph smuggled Lutheran tracts into his homeland. He proved himself one of the most prolific Lutheran pamphleteers and poets of his day. His religious pamphlets and poems touched on every phase of one's life from birth to death: for all occasions in the life of his friends he had words of cheer and comfort. In letters and tracts he admonished his comrades to hold to their religious convictions. His *Trost Lied Eines Exculanten* (Song of Solace for an Exile) reverberated in the ears of millions in the 1730's. Bands of hundreds of Salzburgers marched into cities of Germany amid admiring and cheering throngs singing "I am a poor exile driven from my fatherland for abiding by God's Word." Scheitberger's fervent spiritual conviction can best be judged by what a Catholic historian had to say of him:

In one of his books, the catechism widely circulated in Germany, he showed a lack of understanding of the papacy. Had he been as zealous to inform himself of the Catholic faith, he would not have cast that precious jewel aside.[2]

Max Gandolph, made cardinal a few months preceding his death, distinguished himself as an able administrator, law giver, and economist. His successor as archbishop of Salzburg, John Ernst Thurn (1687-1709), was in no way beholden to the Austrian or the Bavarian dynasty. He was proud, arrogant, and cold in manner, showed an aversion to arduous tasks, but did nevertheless demonstrate an unusual grasp of art, a passion for hunting, a compassion for suffering humanity, an ascetic piety, and a religious fanaticism. It was said of him that, after strenuous fast days, he sought relaxation in the chase or in a game of dice in which he permitted impoverished noblemen to walk away with winnings.

John Ernst, like his predecessors, was called upon to come to the support of the Empire against the Turks and its wars with Louis XIV of France. The threat of a Bavarian invasion into Salzburg necessitated the strengthening of the defenses and expanding the granaries of the capital city. And it was not until the victory of Prince Eugene of Savoy and of General Marlborough that Salzburg was relieved of the Bavarian menace. Salzburg was put to an enormous expense in provisioning the imperial forces on their march to battle through the prince-archbishopric and also for the support of its own contingents in the German army. In 1704, taxes were doubled and a levy was made against every chimney and all alcoholic beverages.

Above all, John Ernst was determined to restore Catholic conformity in his state. Very soon after taking office, he made a tour of the haunts of Protestantism in the uplands. Every immigrant was obliged publicly to profess Catholicism and to pledge to rear his children in that faith. Tradesmen were prohibited from employing non-Catholic apprentices or servants. To prevent smuggling of banned books into the principality, foreign travel and re-entry of travelers were carefully scrutinized. Anyone found to

---

[2]W. Volk, *Die Auswanderung Der Protestantisch Gesinnten Salzburger in Den Jahren* 1731 *u.* 1732. Innsbruck, 1864.

possess heretical books or failing to report their possession was heavily fined. John Ernst established schools for training the clergy and set up pastoral outposts in outlying communities. Ursuline nuns were brought in to teach future mothers, a number of new churches were erected, and monastic foundations were established. The Virgin Mother was proclaimed the patron saint of Salzburg. University professors and public officials were required by oath to subscribe to the doctrine of Immaculate Conception, and take part in religious processions. In 1693, Ernst decreed that any banished person apprehended while secretly returning to see his children was to have his hands riveted to the oars of a galley. A similar penalty was imposed for poaching on the prince-archbishop's hunting preserves.

In 1695 Archbishop Ernst purchased the *Glockenspiel,* carillon, which had been cast in Antwerp for a church in Holland. Ten years later the chimes were mounted in the tower which Ernst had erected for the *Glockenspiel* in 1703. The archbishop's court watchmaker, Jeremiah Sauter, succeeded in mounting and setting up the mechanism for playing the carillon. To this day the daily performance of the *Glockenspiel* is enjoyed by the natives and the throng of tourists who visit the famed city of Salzburg. The expense for this and the operettas staged for the burghers of Salzburg was financed by Ernst's income from his East India Company investment. Everything he did in the way of adding splendor to the city seemed motivated by a desire to appease an insatiable vanity; very little served a useful purpose. By the sweat of their brows the frugal folk of Salzburg were made to bear the financial burden imposed to satisfy the extravagance of a theocratic prelate.

John Ernst's successor, Franz Anton, Count Harrach, bishop and coadjutor of Vienna and archbishop of Salzburg (1709-1727) adopted a somewhat moderate policy toward non-Catholics in a war-torn Europe. In his administration, pietism, a protest against the sterile formalism of the Church and a lack of clerical sincerity, had a very considerable impact on the Salzburgers. In addition to the German Bible, the writings of Johann Arndt and Joseph Scheitberger found their way into the prince-archbishopric. These were circulated from group to group, and, in the secrecy of night, Protestants met to pledge allegiance to the Lutheran Augsburg Confession. Panse wrote that Scheitberger's *Exculantenlied* and his tracts created a stir among the sensitive mountaineers which reminded one of a violent wind surging through the mountain forests of the archbishopric.[3] It was, perhaps, this spiritual revival which contributed in 1731-1734 toward the enthusiastic reception accorded the Lutherans exiled from Salzburg by Archbishop Leopold Anton Eleuterius Freiherr von Firmen (1726-1744).

[3]Karl Panse, *Geschichte der Auswanderung der Evangelischen Salzburger im Jahre* 1732, p. 25.

CHAPTER X

SEVENTEENTH AND EIGHTEENTH CENTURY TRENDS IN SALZBURG

THE SALZBURG prince-archbishops of the seventeenth and eighteenth century were the product of their own European environment. Like the princes of Europe they were set upon the realization of a centralized territorial state and were determined to combat the obstacles which interfered with their ambitious designs. The vast majority of rulers of Europe held to the theory that religious unity was essential to a united and law-abiding state. To enhance their prestige and that of the state, they liberally supported cultural and artistic progress. In an age when the Church was split into violently hostile parties, education of youth assumed greater significance if for no other reason than for the propagation of "The Faith." To satisfy their ambitious designs, like their contemporaries elsewhere, the prince-archbishops of Salzburg drew heavily upon the resources of their diocese. Some of them seemed to wish to outdo their predecessors in the construction, enlargement and beautifying of cathedrals, churches, shrines, and in building hunting lodges, palaces and planning attractive gardens, and parks adjoining their palaces.

Wolf-Dietrich in his seeming vision of making the city of Salzburg the "German Rome" laid the foundation of the archdiocesan cathedral to conform to that of St. Peter's in Rome. Unable to do more than lay the foundation for it, his successor Mark Sittich built it on a smaller scale. In 1628 the work had progressed sufficiently for its dedication by Archbishop Paris Lodron. The Thirty Years' War caused a temporary delay in its completion. Unfortunately the bombing of Salzburg in World War II greatly damaged the beautiful edifice, and its restoration was not completed until 1959. The Cathedral houses one of the largest organs of Europe. It is a real treat to be seated reverently in one of its pews and listen to the music of its more than 3,000 pipes ranging in length from 36 feet to approximately 3 inches. The Cathedral faces a spacious square.

The square bounded by the Cathedral, the residence of the archbishop and other buildings, forms the setting for the Mystery Play "Everyman" which is performed during the annual Salzburg Festival. To the right of the Cathedral is the residence of the archbishop. Dissatisfied with the old structure, Wolf-Dietrich began to rebuild it on a much grander scale to conform to the Cathedral planned by him. Its completion was the work of Franz Anton Harrach (1709-1727), who was responsible for the Italian Renaissance facade of the east front.

Close by the Cathedral is the tower with the *Glockenspiel*. This with the new palace of the archbishop which abuts it, the *Kollegienkirche* (University Church) and the university, help to form the residence square. In the square is the beautiful and impressive Residence Fountain. The *Kollegienkirche* was built in the Austrian Baroque style. At first the university was a kind of high school built by Mark Sittich but in 1623, Paris Lodron reorganized it into a university.

The fortress *Hohensalzburg* was enlarged and improved by Leonhard von Keutschen early in the sixteenth century. The battlements, the inner courtyard with the Chapel of St. Leonhard and the St. George Church of the outer courtyard were the work of Leonhard. During the Thirty Years' War Paris Lodron enlarged the fortifications. The last addition was built by Archbishop Max Gandolph von Kuenburg (1668-1687).

For a diversion from the humdrum of official functions and for the entertainment of prominent guests Mark Sittich, Count von Hohenems, had the Hellbrunn Castle built in a setting of luxurious parks and flower gardens. Sittich, a relative of the papal Medici and for some time a resident of Rome, had come to admire the villas and gardens of that city which inspired his building of Hellbrunn. When informed of the contemplated visit of the Austrian Archduke Maximilian, Grand Master of the Teutonic Knights, Sittich decided hurriedly to go to work with the castle's construction. Within fifteen months this pleasure palace and recreation center was completed on the former sight of a deer-park. Santino Solari, architect for the Cathedral, more than likely planned Hellbrunn and worked as a sculptor for some of the garden statues. Grand Duke Ferdinand II of Tuscany in 1628 said "that Hellbrunn can justly be compared to the most beautiful villas in Italy." Domenico Ghisberti said of it in 1670: "In this park I become even more lost than in a labyrinth. Its waters remind me of Venice, and its buildings make me think of Rome. Hellbrunn is a labyrinth of waters, a play of Naiades, a theater of flowers, a capitol of statues, a museum of the Graces."[1] It is one of the very few country-villas in Europe which has remained as originally built.

From the Castle one passes along the side of a park leading to the open-air theatre crowned by statuary representing Roman victories. Facing it is a table with six stools with an oblong opening in each seat. All but the one at which the host (archbishop) sits have sprays below the seat which can be turned on at the pleasure of the host and the consternation of his guests. From there one passes grotto after grotto containing Greek mythological characters, each with its water sport. Adjoining the group of fountains is the magnificent pleasure garden of gorgeous flower-beds and two big ponds surrounded by statuary.

Martin, in his *Hellbrunn Castle,* wrote:

> A direct connection exists between the waterworks at Hellbrunn and those described in a book published in Frankfurt in 1615 by Salomon de Caus. In both these cases the original stimulus must be looked for in Italy.
>
> The park is particularly interesting for the student of art. The Grotto of Ruins brings to mind that cult of artificial ruins which first showed itself one and a half centuries later, and the hermitages anticipate the sentimental nature worship of the Romantic Age. In all this we can already discern the two contrasting poles of the Baroque Age — on the one side a love of pleasure and on the other, asceticism.
>
> No better evidence of the ambiguous character of the ecclesiastical rulers of that time exists than in Hellbrunn Castle itself. In the city of a morning, Marcus Sittius was the devout prelate, who founded monastical fraternities, and whose cowl he wore when taking part in their processions which he himself had ordered. In the afternoon, he became a worldly prince, refusing to occupy himself with ecclesiastical affairs and giving himself up to the pleasures of the senses. Such a manifestation of a two-sided personality can be only understood in the light of the Baroque spirit.[2]

[1]Franz Martin, *Hellbrunn Castle*, (Salzburg, 1957), p. 728.
[2]Martin, *Hellbrunn Castle*, pp. 32 and 33.

By the middle of the eighteenth century, the Salzburg Landtag (assembly of estates) had ceased to function as a deliberative body. Being subject to the call of the prince-archbishop, it was convened only in times of crisis to place its stamp of approval on decrees propounded and formulated by him. The first and second estates, clergy and nobility, were only too willing to forgo their part in affairs of state in return for recognition of their inherited medieval privilege of exemption from taxes. All efforts on the part of the burgher class, subject to a steadily mounting tax burden, to retain a part in government failed. At the same time, local officials appointed by the hierarchical administrators tenaciously held to their source of income derived from fines. In fact, the constant threat of attack in a war-torn Europe tended to increase their numbers and enhance their power.

During this period the general moral standard of the Salzburgers was at a low ebb. In 1679, Max Gandolph ordered heavy fines and imprisonment at hard labor, even banishment, for fornication and adultery. John Ernst, to strike at the root of these evils ten years later, ordered minor offenders of the moral code publicly pilloried. Such things as loitering in streets, nocturnal visits by lovers before the bedchamber windows of their ladies, and dancing from May 3 to September 14 were prohibited. Franz Anton, about a quarter century later, ordered that men- and maid-servants be made to occupy separate sleeping quarters.

Many efforts were made by various archbishops to improve the ethical standards and instill respect for elders in the children. To encourage respect for parents in their children, the latter were to be told to refrain from the use of the familiar form of *du* and use the polite form *Sie* when addressing a parent. All attempts to prevent the use of tobacco and snuff having failed, an excise tax equal to their cost was levied against these luxuries. Games of chance and the carrying of weapons were prohibited. John Ernst, in failing in an effort to prevent begging and seeking alms on the public streets of the capital, made the care of the indigent a community responsibility. Foreign beggars were ordered ejected from the principality, and gypsies were outlawed. Able-bodied women-beggars who failed to find employment were placed in a workhouse or banished. Rigid regulations issued by Max Gandolph against minor infractions failed to put an end to brawls of students, soldiers, apprentices, and servants. In May, 1675, only the personal intervention by the archbishop prevented bloodshed in an armed clash of students and soldiers. The gaiety and splendor of the princely household and the superficial display of intellectual attainment on the part of the university students failed to conceal the decadent character of society that was so characteristic of the states of Germany at this time.

Imposing structures were built to provide for elaborate entertainments befitting a prince of Salzburg. Archbishop Lang, in the era of the Reformation, built a banquet hall large enough for thirty tables. Ernst, his successor, had two halls vaulted and joined with it the large residence hall of the Chaplain. To make certain that his household and guests would not want for grain, bins were enlarged, and a bakery, a brew house, a blacksmith shop, and servant residences were constructed. Archbishop Michael constructed a tall watchtower from which a watchman sounded a bell at quarter-hour intervals. On festal days a bell was rung for dining, and on other days a trumpet was sounded. In 1573, the expense for entertainment at court amounted to more than 100,000 Kronen[3] and more than 3,787 casks of wine and 1,365 pails of beer were consumed. An average of 264 persons per meal dined at court expense twice daily; many of these guests were prominent nobles and their retainers.

All attempts on the part of the Cathedral Chapter to encourage less expensive and elaborate entertainment failed. Great pomp was exhibited at the entertainment of foreign princes. At Halloween in 1558 and again in 1568, when Albrecht of Bavaria and Karl of Stiermark respectively arrived with a large following, no fewer than 750 horses had to be provided for them. One of the attendants was most eloquent in his description of the elaborate decoration of the prelate's residence of the gorgeous basilica of St. Rupert and of the relics of Salzburg saints set in gold and jewels.

By the close of the seventeenth century, Salzburg was no longer dependent upon Italian craftsmen as architects, sculptors, stucco workers, and painters. The archbishopric could pride itself on having able builders and masons, capable sculptors, painters, and many highly skilled artisans. The outstanding architect, John Bernhard von Erlach, could depend upon these to give form to his imaginative structural plans.

---

[3] J. Dye, *Coin Encyclopedia* (1883), p. 640. Krone = $2.38.

In spite of its outward splendor, Salzburg was confronted by a steady economic decline. Public beggars in the city and the countryside increased. With rosary in hand they gathered at the archbishop's residence, the city gate, and the cathedral. The expense of the bishop's almsgiving ran well over 100,000 Gulden. Equally as expensive were the widows' pensions borne by the communities in which they resided. At the end of the seventeenth century, the economy of Salzburg was suffering severely. The princely splendor of the capitalist mine-owning families, the Weitmosers, the Feuersengers, had long since vanished. The mining operations of Gastein had almost come to a halt, and no longer were the Gastein workmen the jovial lads of yesterday. Only the salt mining industry was spared an economic collapse. Fortunately, the plight of the peasantry was less serious. Many were very comfortably situated, their servants were well treated, and there was for them no scarcity of food in spite of an increasing population.

All efforts to stimulate employment through a regulation of commerce and industry failed. The sale of leather imports was prohibited, and peasants were forbidden to tan their own leather. The grinding of grain was to be paid for in money rather than in kind. All wood structures or repairs were restricted to bonafide carpenters. Peasants who had been in the habit of doing their own carpentering, tanning hides of their stock for leather, grinding their own grain or paying for it in kind, rebelled against the bishop's orders. But all requests for relief were ignored. In 1702, when John Ernst had completed his glass works at Huettenstein, glass imports were prohibited. In spite of precautionary measures against smuggling, the influx of contraband goods increased.

CHAPTER XI

THE DIE IS CAST

AT NO TIME since Luther, had an archbishop of Salzburg been in a more favorable position to achieve religious unity for his principality than was Leopold Anton von Firmian (1727-1741). Protestants of Germany, split into hostile factions, were fighting a losing battle with a reformed, rejuvenated, and militant Catholic Church. The feud within Protestant ranks, in particular between sterile, dogmatic confessionalists and the pietists who stressed Christ-like living rather than dogma and creed, was causing doubt and a return to the Catholic fold on the part of many Protestants. Universities like Heidelberg had fallen to Catholic leadership. Princes and nobles who found an advantage in changing their outer garment of religion did so without the slightest scruple. The Elector of Saxony, once the outstanding champion of Lutheranism, had no hesitancy in professing the Catholic faith when the throne of Poland seemed within his grasp. Even Protestant theologians hesitated to speak out in defense of their convictions, while still others declared publicly that they found little difference in basic Catholic and Protestant doctrines.

Though the immediate threat of attack upon Germany seemed to have been dispelled in the second decade of the eighteenth century through the defeat of Louis XIV of France in the War of the Spanish Succession (1701-1713), and through the defeat of the Turks by Prince Eugene of Savoy at Belgrade in 1717, the weak internal structure of the German Empire was such as to enable Archbishop Firmian to do as he pleased in ridding his principality of Lutheran dissent. All attempts on the part of the German emperor to institute administrative reforms which would make for greater unity in times of foreign aggression came to naught through the menace of power politics involving the numerous princes of the Empire. The paramount concern of Emperor Charles VI (1711-

1740) was to secure the acceptance of his Pragmatic Sanction[1] by the rulers of Europe and the German princes, including Firmian. Through it he hoped to circumvent the terms of the Salic Law providing succession to his crown through a male heir by having his daughter Maria Theresa succeed him to the throne.

The status of the Empire was such as to insure Firmian of considerable freedom in coming to grips with Protestantism in his principality. When he assumed office he found the seat of government, the city of Salzburg, fairly free from heresy. On the other hand, religious dissent was far greater in the rural area than he realized. Here the Catholics, whose economic and political grievances were no different from those of the Protestants, frequently closed ranks with them. The freedom-loving peasants and mountaineers held the church hierarchy responsible for their economic plight and rebelled against the steady encroachment of ultramontane Italian cultural influence upon their Germanic environment.

Catholic Tyrolese Italians had gradually edged the native German population northward. Old German cultural lore was being blocked through Italian infiltration. The popular German sagas of *Dietrich von Bern* of *Wieland* and others were being forced to make way for the lives of saints. The imposition of Latin liturgical forms in religious services was deeply resented. The contrast was most important in the city of Salzburg, where Italian influence had reached an ascendant position and where, above all, the spiritual and temporal prince was steeped in Italian ultramontanism, domination from beyond the mountains. The slogan of the German mountain folk was "Freedom from Rome." They held to their demand for German sermons and sacramental ritual, and rebelled against the confiscation of their German Bibles and highly cherished Lutheran tracts.

In contrast, the administrators of Salzburg from 1727 to 1741 were zealous Catholics bred in the Jesuit tradition of thoroughness. They believed that the end justifies the means. Firmian, von Roell, and the shrewd Machiavellian Cristani seemed to be passionate disciples of the doctrine that the Catholic Church alone possesses the true teaching of Christ. They claimed that it was founded by

---

[1]This was an agreement sought by Charles VI, Holy Roman Emperor, whereby the princes of the empire would not oppose the succession of his daughter, Maria Theresa, to Charles' dominions.

Christ and that through the ages under the guidance of its founder it cannot err. To them a Catholic prelate in whom spiritual and temporal power was vested owes it to the flock entrusted to him to eradicate what might endanger its salvation.

Leopold (Anton Eleutherius) Freiherr von Firmian was born May 27, 1679. He was named Leopold for his godfather Leopold I. His father was then a deputy of the empire at Munich. He received his education at a Jesuit Gymnasium and later served as a page at the court of John Ernst, Archbishop of Salzburg. At the age of fifteen he went to Rome to continue his education at the Collegium Germanicum, founded by Ignatius Loyola. Here he studied Canon Law and Dialectics. Upon the completion of his studies in Rome he returned to Salzburg, where he was appointed to the Cathedral Chapter. Throughout his career the influence of his Italian and Jesuit training was ever evident. He was far better versed in the art of Italian politics and diplomacy than in German affairs. In 1718 he was chosen Bishop of Lavant and in 1724 to a similar office of Seckau, near Graz in the archbishopric of Salzburg. Practically all of his years preceding his appointment to the office of prince-archbishop of Salzburg he resided at Graz, the seat of a famous Jesuit University. His Graz associates were the members of the College of the Society of Jesus. Firmian was a scholar, proud, hardhearted, a loyal Jesuit of stern countenance, devoted to wine and the chase.

The elevation of Leopold Anton von Firmian to the office of Archbishop was more or less an accident. Unable to reach an agreement, the Salzburg Cathedral Chapter hit upon Firmian as a compromise candidate. But, alas, no sooner had he been consecrated than his health showed a marked improvement and, to the dismay of his appointers, he was able to round out a fairly long and eventful career. The 100,000 Thalers (approximately $75,000) which he paid to secure the appointment and the pallium was assessed against the treasury of the prince-archbishopric.

Few prelates of Salzburg served the principality as poorly as he. His contemporaries found him to be an unsociable, haughty, and cold upstart. In addition to a passion for religious unity, he reveled in the chase and was captivated by the adulation of his hunting companions. Like many of his predecessors in office and contemporaries, he believed that fiscal affairs of the state were matters of private concern and that therefore the public treasury

85

could be plundered for the support of his relatives. One of his first utterances after his appointment as archbishop was an expression of his ambition to restore the Catholic Church to all its splendor in Salzburg. To this end, he promised to emulate Philip of Spain (1556-1598), who so successfully had rid Spain and his empire of "heresy." The historian Hanke said that he was Tyrolese with little sympathy for German institutions and customs. Surrounded by Catholic favorites, among them a woman who helped to formulate his policies, he was keenly interested in insuring his own well-being and that of his relatives. To that end he drew on the resources of the prime-archbishopric and confiscated the land of "heretics" for the enrichment of the impoverished members of his family.

In all of the provinces there was yet no thought of rebellion. A love for hearth and home far outweighed any resentment against the steadily mounting fiscal exactions for spiritual and secular needs. Fines, which were designed chiefly for purposes of revenue, were far out of proportion to the offences committed, no matter how trivial the infraction might be. This situation, like the banishment and imprisonment of Lutheran leaders in underground dungeons, was accepted as more or less inevitable. A general feeling of better days to come seemed to pervade the atmosphere.

The placid scene suddenly erupted into violent protest at the unexpected announcement that members of the Jesuit Order were to be brought in to rid the country of religious dissent. All previous prelates contemplating a similar goal refused to call upon the assistance of the Society of Jesus. They knew full well the possible consequence of inviting the assistance of men despised and feared alike by the rank and file of the people and the monks of Salzburg, particularly the Benedictines. That the spontaneous outburst against Firmian's course was part of a plot hatched by German princes to place Salzburg under a Protestant was unfounded. Equally flimsy was the claim that secret agents working out of Berlin and Dresden had gone into the uplands of Salzburg to incite a rebellion aimed at establishing a republic like that of Switzerland. Firmian and his confidential advisers refused to permit their carefully laid plan to be interrupted. No more than ten Jesuits were to be brought into Salzburg at a time. Independent of the priesthood they were ordered more firmly "to ground the loyal Catholics" in their faith, and to guide the wayward souls back into the fold. However, it was soon apparent to them that the doctrines of Luther had been handed down by word of mouth from parents to children, from generation to generation, in most of the mountain communities. Jesuits who were sent south to Gastein, nestled in the enchanting foothills of the Alps, complained that hardly a family was free of heresy. Little had been done by previous administrations to disturb the Lutheran workers in the salt mines whose salt production was a lucrative source of income for the archbishop.

Under the pretext of a pastoral call, a churchman accompanied by a civilian officer was to enter the homes where anyone was suspected of being a Protestant. Promptly the premises were searched for censored literature. Naturally, such inquisitive procedure could hardly be expected to escape some form of verbal remonstrance from persons the sanctity of whose homes was thus being violated. Frequently the unwelcome guests were ordered to leave to avoid being thrown out. One housewife was so enraged that she called the intruder a Catholic heretic and the Pope a perverter of the Scriptures and of men, then without further ado showed him the door. For such and similar infractions, offenders were cited to account for their conduct at a specified mission station.

To placate and publicly expose the Protestants, all Salzburgers were ordered to greet each other publicly in the following manner: "Praised be Jesus Christ," and to respond, "Forever, Amen." Everyone was to wear the "Scapular," a medallion blessed by a priest, hanging exposed from about the neck. This requirement was ignored and denounced by the Lutherans as a form of idolatry. In defiance of orders to the contrary, Protestant conventicles were held and non-Catholic literature continued to be read and smuggled across the border under camisoles, in crocks and small barrels.

With the failure of a policy of moderation and peaceful persuasion, more drastic measures were adopted. Wayward persons were publicly excommunicated, and persons in possession of censored literature were imprisoned. Hans Lercher and Viet Breme were placed in irons and confined in an underground dungeon for weeks and then banished. Their property was confiscated and was claimed to be applied to the support of wife and children. Appeals on behalf of the banished victims by the *Corpus Evangelicorum,* an organization of Protestant princes of the German Reichstag at Ratisbon, demanding that the victims' loved ones be reunited with them, was ignored. The search and seizure of banned literature continued and the slightest religious infraction was severely punished.

In a carefully devised plan the lieutenants of Firmian, von Roell and Cristani, set out to draw more sharply the line of cleavage between Protestant and Catholic and to expose the non-Catholics who publicly conformed to the ritual of the Roman Church. All worshipers were ordered to pray the beads of the Rosary in public view while in Church, to participate in all religious processions, of which there were many, and to make pilgrimages to holy places. A priest who showed the slightest evidence of a sympathetic understanding of a parishioner was forthwith displaced by one ready to enforce the mandate of Firmian. To obtain desired confessions, recantation of heresy and to intimidate the wayward, prisoners were chained to blocks and thrown into foul underground dungeons into which no light penetrated. "Fortunately," an order of 1704 specified that the dungeon be cleaned twice a year and the victim be furnished a blanket. To escape the horrors of such an ordeal it was a common practice for peasants to be noncommittal and pretend ignorance in religious matters. Persons who failed to report religious infractions were severely punished. All news to the outside world was censored and the frontier was closed to Protestant entrants and heretical literature was prohibited from being brought in.

An appeal signed by 19,000 peasants of Pongau province who resided in the administrative districts of *Radstadt, Wagrin, Werfen, Bischofshofen, St. Johann,* and *Gastein* was formally delivered to the *Corpus Evangelicorum* at Ratisbon, something unheard of in the annals of Salzburg history. This shocked Firmian into realizing the magnitude of the task he had set out to accomplish. In this appeal the signers blamed the numerous and long imprisonments, and the excessive fines imposed by ignorant and fanatical clergy had aroused resentment toward the government of Salzburg. The peasants were incensed by the Sunday sermon of the vicar of Groszarler who, much like the minister of St. John's church, stormed and fumed in his Sunday sermons. In spite of an order to remain calm, he completely ignored the Gospel and instead viciously and slanderously denounced Luther. It would have surprised no one, they said, had his remarks brought on a public commotion. In the petition they requested either religious freedom or the privilege to emigrate without interference.[2]

Zillberger, the representative of Salzburg at the Diet, had on occasions sharply criticized the policy of Firmian and proposed that he follow the example of the Apostle Paul. Instead of prison walls he advised moderation and patience. Not until the Pongau petition of the 19,000 peasants was made public did he become reconciled to the policy pursued by the archbishop.

In response to the report and mounting criticism, the government of Salzburg ordered a survey to ascertain the general temper of the mountain folk. The investigation commission was ordered to proceed cautiously and do nothing that would incite resentment or violence. A desperate effort was made to allay suspicion. Local officers who were generally disliked were prohibited from having a part in the study and were not to be present at an investigation. The quiet cooperation of the peasants contradicted all rumors that violence was imminent in the uplands, and in no case did an investigator find it necessary to call for police protection. The survey, which was begun on Sunday, July 15, 1731, was completed and the findings delivered to Firmian on July 30.

The study group found religious grievances to be comparatively slight. Its report did, on the other hand, condemn the oppressive and offensive tactics of spiritual as well as political officials. Though Protestants were firm in their faith and were not inclined to yield in matters of conscience, they were reported to be loyal citizens in every other respect. In the district of Werfen resentment was quite pronounced against an increase in death and burial charges and the heavier taxes collected from the wood lands, Though they found the number of loyal supporters of the Protestant faith to be greater than they expected and there seemed to them no immediate cause for alarm, they advised the stationing of 150 regular soldiers at Radstadt to act as a stabilizing influence in the nearby area.

In spite of the encouraging report, Firmian was determined to abide by his decision to return the "erring lambs to the Catholic fold." The serene atmosphere soon erupted into a storm of resentment when von Roell publicly announced on July 30, 1731, that all

[2]Joseph Karl Meyer, *Die Emigration der Prot. Salzburger*, *in Mitteilung der Geschichte fur Salzburger Landeskunde*, LXX, 10 (Franz Martin, editor, Salzburg 1930.)

Pfleger (local officials) were to prohibit the holding of public meetings, pending further orders from the archbishop. At the same time, peasants and mountain folk were assured that all troop movements to strategic positions were precautionary and defensive measures to guard against outside attack. Such an assurance could hardly be taken lightly by the Lutherans when on August 4, all Catholics were alerted to prepare themselves against a sudden attack. This was followed by the recruiting of 500 musketeers and the enrollment of all able-bodied reserves for military service at one-half of the regular pay. Two days later, Cristani, confident of von Roell, organized and assumed personal command of a body of Catholic deputies.

The militant action of the administration and the malicious rumors circulated so aroused the Protestants of the uplands as to provoke their adoption of security measures. Some of the more outspoken agitators went so far as to propose taking up arms and raiding public arsenals. Some of the less vociferous met secretly at Schwarzach on August 5, and chose delegates to present a petition to the Imperial Diet at Ratisbon asking for military protection. This petition, presented by the three who escaped arrest and imprisonment in Salzburg, was ignored by the Diet. In the months which followed there was a steady increase in the number of rumors and false charges that Protestants had gone to the doors of Catholics and threatened to attack them and set fire to their homes, should they fail to take up arms in their behalf. They wondered why soldiers should be quartered in Radstadt, a town with few Lutherans. Rumor, however, had it that the Catholics of that community were in danger of death at the hands of the non-Catholics. Such charges were circulated when antagonism between Catholic and Protestant had reached a climax in the Reichstag. The non-Catholic members seemed at that time to want to make of that representative body of the Empire a kind of forum in which Catholic members could be made to account for acts of their governments.

The liberty-loving and hospitable men of the uplands, who on the surface were rough-and-ready and given to strong language, could hardly be expected to accept calmly the false charges hurled at them and other Lutherans. During the months of ferment many a wild threat was made by some of them. But, in spite of all the hue and cry, no one thought of open revolt as feared by Firmian and his lieutenants. None the less, he could hardly be ignorant of the imminent danger once faced by Archbishop Matthew Lang during the Peasants' War of 1525, when he was obliged to retreat to the fortress *Hohensalzburg* and hold out for weeks until relieved by the archduke of Bavaria.

In the face of Protestant threats, for which he was largely responsible, Firmian requested Emperor Charles VI to furnish imperial troops for maintaining order in Salzburg. When the emperor failed to respond promptly, the archbishop forced his hand by negotiating with the archduke of Bavaria. On August 16, 1731, the emperor acceded to the archbishop's request, but specified that the troops were not to engage in military attacks nor was any blood to be shed by them. Preceding the arrival of the first contingent of 200 cavalrymen and 1000 foot-soldiers, the archbishop made the public announcement that family devotionals without sermons and attended by friends would be permitted. In no instance, however, were more than three Protestants at a time to meet at a prearranged place.

Defiant reaction to this by the non-Catholics was not long delayed. In the rural communities, posters which announced this order were ridiculed and destroyed, and the general confusion and excitement was such as to afford Firmian ample reason for urging the emperor to act without delay before matters got out of hand. In his appeal to a hesitant emperor he complained that the peasantry proved itself more defiant from day to day, that they were holding religious services, were conducting funerals without benefit of clergy, and were audaciously ridiculing the saints. With the arrival of soldiers came an imperial manifesto which called upon the aroused populace of Salzburg to refrain from violence and upon the archbishop to conform to the laws of the Empire, to comply with the religious provisions of the Treaty of Westphalia, which laid down the procedure to be followed before banishing Protestants, and to ease the burdens of his people. This manifesto was suppressed by Firmian.

From time to time after September 22, 1731, troops who moved into the principality of Salzburg with the least possible fanfare were strategically placed. The cavalry was stationed in the lowlands, and the foot soldiers were deployed into the mountain hamlets. That they were quartered alike in Catholic and non-Catholic homes was categorically denied by the Protestants. The first of the contingent to arrive was the cavalry commanded by Prince Eugene, hero of the Turkish war and an ambitious politician. From the outset he adopted a moderate and tolerant policy. Six of his fifteen officers and one hundred of his seven hundred and seventy-four men were Lutheran. His apparent sympathy for Lutherans within the area of his command prompted Firmian to request the withdrawal of the cavalry because their presence was no longer necessary in the lowlands. The total number of troops eventually quartered in the principality was conservatively estimated to have been between two and three thousand, certainly too few to deal with the rumored rebellious situation.

Once the troops had been deployed satisfactorily, a directive was circulated calling for a firmer policy by all local officials. In it they were told that the temperate policy of the archbishop had been defied with abandon. In response to orders, the *Pfleger* secretly arrested and gagged Protestant leaders, put them on horseback, or packed them in carts held in readiness, and rushed them to the city of Salzburg for imprisonment in the fortress. In the meantime, the loyal supporters of Firmian were ordered to the defense of the city until the militia could take over. Between October 8 and 15, Protestant leaders from all parts of the principality were rushed to the capital city. To prevent word of what was happening from reaching the *Collegium Evangelicorum,* the college of Protestant deputies of the German Diet, an effort was made to close the frontier. Not until November 5, 1731, was the Prussian representative well enough informed to be able to advise Frederick William I, King of Prussia, of developments in Salzburg.

Word of the arrests evoked a passionate resentment on the part of the confederates of the prisoners. They called for a secret meeting to plan ways and means of liberating the prisoners before they could be incarcerated in the fortress at Salzburg. In some areas the disturbance was such as to necessitate guards being kept on the alert both day and night. At Ratisbon, the seat of the representatives of the Empire, protests were filed condemning the brutal treatment of Protestant leaders. Firmian was accused of refusing to grant the prisoners a trial, of detaining the children of refugees, and of seizing and confiscating refugee property on the pretext that the proceeds were to be used for the support of children who were said to have refused to join their parents. The complaint likewise held the archbishop responsible for the violation of the law of the land and the terms of the treaty of Westphalia. This was categorically denied by Firmian, who informed the emperor that the sole purpose of his acts was the suppression of rebellion. From now on, to escape the charge that he was violating the Treaty of Westphalia, he stressed his need for putting down violence and suppressing rebellion.

Once the known Protestant leaders had been imprisoned, the disarming of their confederates was ordered. A secret directive sent to local officers on October 16 called for a registration of all guards, indicating their marital status and the character of their equipment. This, it was noted, was made necessary by the prevailing crisis. On the morning of October 22, every armed guard was to report fully equipped to his local officer. Should he fail to report he was subject to a fine of one hundred *Reichsthaler,* or banishment in case the fine was not paid. The muster-roll was to contain the total number of commissioned officers and men. Upon dismissal each should hold himself in readiness to report for duty at a moment's notice.

A part of the order cloaked in secrecy called upon the imperial forces to make sure that the guards reported. If necessary, they were to make a house-to-house canvas, and to note any adverse response to their call.

On the pretext of a maneuver, the imperial forces were assembled at their respective headquarters fully armed and with their muskets loaded for action. The next morning, in veiled secrecy, they were to divide the local guards into two groups, making sure that all known and suspected Lutherans were in the one and Catholics in the other. As soon as the classification had been completed, the former were to be surrounded and disarmed by the soldiers. After having been given a receipt for their guns they were told these would either be returned, or the arms not returned would be paid for. On the other hand, loyal Catholic *Schuetzen* (local guards) were to retain their firearms. In the process all resentful deeds and words were to be recorded. In spite of the unusual procedure everything passed off without incident. In his report to Emperor Charles VI, Friday, October 26, Firmian advised him that matters had calmed down since the appearance of the imperial forces and that the rebels appeared calmer and more submissive. Unfortunately, this by no means meant that incitement to violence had suddenly ended.

Having convinced the emperor of the imminence of violence in parts of Salzburg, Firmian then sought to vitiate the charge of the Protestant princes of the Empire, that he had violated the religious provisions of the Peace of Westphalia. He therefore dispatched Catholic priests to visit the homes of suspected Lutherans and to catechize them on the doctrines set forth in the Augsburg Confession of the Lutheran Church. As might be expected, the interrogations reported that the purported Lutherans had no knowledge of the basic doctrines of their church, and that their leaders were unable to establish the Scriptural truth of the doctrines which they taught.

Rumors of threats of violence and the possibility of a Protestant revolt in the rural and mountain districts seemed to pose a real menace to the seat of the principality, the city of Salzburg, where so-called heresy was almost nonexistent. Here it was generally felt that the seditious "poison" of Lutheranism, if allowed to spread unchecked, might bring about the secularization of all church property in the principality. If at all possible, Firmian would far rather have crushed the movement. However, realizing the impossibility of this after July, 1731, he concluded that his only alternative was to expel the non-Catholics forcibly at the earliest possible opportunity.

The first proposal for mass emigration was proposed in a petition signed by the nineteen thousand peasants of Pongau. In it they asked to be allowed to liquidate their holdings and depart peaceably as guaranteed by the terms of Westphalia, hoping, of course, that such a proposal would have a sobering effect on Firmian rather than be accepted at its face value. Unfortunately, they had not fathomed the inflexible determination of Firmian to leave no stone unturned to do for Salzburg what Philip II had done for Spain. To add insult to injury, over one hundred peasants met at a prearranged place at the break of day. Gathered about a barrel of salt, they offered up a joint prayer and took the "salt pledge." Before disbanding each lapped the salt in the barrel as a symbol of unending loyalty to one another. From then on they shunned all Catholic services. In a tense situation such as this the scene as enacted by the Schwarzachers could hardly be expected to take on the air of a prayer meeting.

By September the religious crisis and the accompanying turmoil had reached a point at which the order for the expulsion of "heretics" and "rebels" could be justified in a formal decree, the *Emigrationspatent*. Although couched in the language of a sovereign prince of the Empire, this decree issued by Firmian could by no means disregard the emperor and ignore the *Corpus Evangelicorum*. In the preface its author, more than likely Cristani, attempted skillfully to forestall any attack on the decree by the *Corpus* in the German *Reichstag*. On the basis of events since July, Firmian made sure of clearing himself of any wrongdoing and expressed his intention to weed out certain "boisterous and disloyal" characters. He accused them of peddling malicious falsehoods to the Diet and emphatically declared that their conduct deprived them of any right to property or to life and limb, which was being allowed in the terms of the Patent. Firmian insisted that the arrest and imprisonment of rebellious leaders on September 28 had no religious significance. He charged that they were inciting to insurrection in Salzburg and were enlisting neighboring counties to take up arms in their behalf. He claimed, further, that they would not have hesitated to incite a religious war which could have inflamed the Holy Roman Empire.

On October 29, 1731, the Archbishop of Salzburg, by means of the *Emigrationspatent,* confronted Charles VI with a *fait accompli*. Two days later, on All Saints Day, 1731, commemorating the anniversary of the Reformation and the date when Luther tacked his ninety-five theses on the door of the Castle Church of Wittenberg, Firmian affixed his signature to the *Emigrationspatent*. Five days later, on the birthday of the reformer, it was sent to every district in the principality, to be made public on Luther's baptismal date, November 11, 1731.

In the interim between November 5 and 11, local officers were directed to make a diligent search of the homes of all but known Catholics for weapons still held in defiance of previous orders. Within three days all guns (rifles, shotguns, pistols, and any other form of projector), grenades, sabers, swords, bayonets, daggers, stilettos, and medieval cudgels were to be surrendered. Persons failing to comply were subject to summary punishment. Almost without exception, the search was executed without incident or the slightest protest. Only one person, the "arch heretic" Hans Hofgaertner, baker of *Bischofshofen,* declared that he would have his rifles forged into one piece rather than surrender them.

On the fateful November 11, the populace of each Salzburg community was ordered to assemble and listen to a reading of the *Emigrationspatent*. The introduction, which was a lengthy harangue extolling the magnanimity of Firmian and condemning the criminal and rebellious conduct of the Protestants, was followed by the merciless decree of expulsion. Each and every professed Lutheran or Evangelical (Calvinist) subject who held no real property was ordered to leave, bag and baggage, within eight days of the publication of the decree. Included in the order were all self-employed workers, day laborers, men- and maid-servants over twelve years of age. Persons who failed to obey were subject to severe punishment. Exception would be made of the ones who would forthwith agree to return to the Catholic fold and give specific proof of their sincerity within fifteen days. All employees of the archbishop in his mining and salt industries or in any other capacity were to be dismissed immediately and their wages were to cease with the publication of the decree, and no one was to be employed in their stead if he were devotee of the proscribed faiths. Real-property holders were to be allowed from one to three months in which to dispose of their property, depending on its assessed value. All local officials were diligently to execute the order and put in chains anyone who failed to comply. If necessary, they were to call on the militia for aid. They were at the same time warned not to permit themselves to be swayed by friendship, hatred or bribery.

CHAPTER XII

CONSTERNATION, ANXIETY, DOUBT, FEAR, HOPE

ALL THOSE affected by the fateful and ruthless terms of the publicly posted and publicly read *Emigrationspatent* of November 11, 1731, were stunned and temporarily rendered speechless. They were overcome by a feeling of gloom and doom as it dawned on them that in a matter of days, they were to be expelled and at a time when the rigors of winter were closing in on them. It was all too apparent to them that Firmian's promise, which preceded the survey which had been made of the general status of his subjects in July, 1731, was but a pretense designed to throw the Lutherans off guard. This promise to lighten or abolish their grievances, in the manner of a "kindly father of his country," was a trick to make it less difficult for him to single out his Lutheran "children." Neighborly friendships between Catholic, if found associating with a "rebellious" Protestant heretic, exposed him to possible criticism and even insult.

In the calmer moments which followed the paralyzing shock inflicted by the ruthless terms of the Patent its victims were given to a rationalizing process. Some found the order so shocking as to doubt that it could or would be enforced as outlined. Others wishfully theorized that Firmian's primary objective was to frighten them into a recanting of their faith. Still others, recalling the policy of the archbishop's predecessors, believed that expediency would dictate a more reasonable policy. This opinion was held by the many workers in the salt mine of the Duerrnberg at Hallein. Little therefore was done to prepare for the inevitable day of doom. Those fortunate enough to have Bibles, religious tracts, or copies of sermons looked to them for comfort.

Already the higher mountain peaks were wrapped in a glistening white winter mantle. From this region of snow and ice frigid storms began to sweep down into the peaceful valleys below. Anticipation of winter holidays with their sports and amusements in nature's wonderland gave way to foreboding. The waking hours must have been haunted by the thought of having to trudge along day after day through the numbing snow and slough, not knowing where their next meal would come from, or where to rest their weary heads by night. Even the quiet of the night afforded them little or no relief. Confronted by inestimable trials, the non-propertied, first to be expelled, made a final appeal for a stay of their departure until spring. The extra eight days' delay granted because of Firmian's failure to secure for them the right to travel through neighboring states merely brought the victims closer to the rigors of winter.

On the verge of despair, three hundred persons without passes sought to take flight from Salzburg. By night they hurried northward toward Radstadt, pursued by the military, and legend has it that they were guided through a treacherous terrain by a ray of light while the soldiers in pursuit were shrouded in darkness. On their way northward to Radstadt a beam of light resembling lightning pointed the approach to a bridge across the river Ens. One of the soldiers who witnessed the "miraculous" phenomenon was so frightened as to exclaim: "Either God or the devil is with them. I will have nothing to do with them." Unfortunately, the three hundred were stopped in a principality bordering on Salzburg, held as robbers, and then returned to Salzburg at the point of bayonets. The deep snow through which they were obliged to flounder was colored crimson by their blood. At Salzburg the survivors were consolidated with one of the first contingents to be expelled.

They encountered little sympathy among the population of the almost exclusively Catholic city of Salzburg. Here they were denounced as "damned heretics," to which they responded: "Since you lack the ability to create, you are without the power to damn." Without the necessary means of support, they were forced to seek what shelter they could find against the cold in stables and barns.

Of the groups assembled in the city of Salzburg, a few lost courage and thirty-six of them returned to the old church. However, in spite of all attempts at intimidation, one thousand remained faithful to their convictions. One by one they were taken into one of the courts of the fortress *Hohensalzburg* in full view of blood-stained walls. In this gruesome surrounding each was entreated to denounce his faith and return to the fold of the only true church of Christ or to die as had his brothers. In spite of the graphic description of the horrors they faced if they refused to renounce their Protestant faith, they held fast to their convictions.

To return to the Catholic fold, one was required to take an oath of loyalty to the Catholic Church, to renounce Lutheranism as a heresy and a damning faith, and to accept the tenet that through Catholic Doctrine alone could one be saved. One must agree that the Mass was a sacrificial offering for the living and the dead, and must also assent to the basic doctrine that no one can be saved without the intercession of the Virgin Mary and the saints. One also had to subscribe to a belief in the existence of purgatory as a place where the soul can do penance for its sins and thus be restored to God's grace and enter heaven; one must agree that Holy Communion in the form of one element, bread, has greater value than that of two elements, bread and wine; and one must accept the doctrine that one is saved, not through faith alone (a Lutheran and Calvinist doctrine), but through faith and good works.

In many instances local and military personnel were so shocked by the inhuman procedure as to procrastinate in enforcing the decree. They had to be goaded into action and were told to show neither sympathy nor mercy and to hasten the process by making an example of the more recalcitrant individuals. Many of them declared that if they had deserved punishment they would gladly live and die in their homeland. The one thing they would not do was to revoke the Evangelical faith.

Henchmen accompanied by soldiers entered the homes of non-propertied Lutherans and, amidst much excitement, found the occupants, regardless of age, sex, or physical handicaps, and forcibly herded them to designated centers of concentration. Some of the propertied Lutherans, who were upset by the loss of their employees among those seized, ignored efforts made to detain them until spring, and decided to salvage what they could, and leave the principality along with their tenants and servants. As they traveled on, they gladly shared their means of support.

Whenever a considerable number were driven from their homes, confusion was boundless. Men, women and children embraced each other as they bade adieu. Landlords and their families cast aside all formality and fondly embraced their tenants, servants and their families as they took leave of them. Many of the landlords who were not permitted to leave until the next spring voiced the fond hope for a reunion in a new land of refuge. Catholic members of Protestant households were so impressed by the crusading spirit which prevailed as to profess adherence to the Lutheran faith, so that they might take leave with their kith, kin, and neighbors. In fact, some Catholics were so overcome emotionally as to want to join the crusade. In some villages the urge to follow along had gained such a momentum that armed guards were needed to restrain Catholics from leaving their homeland.

The expulsion was commenced in the village of Werfen in Pongau province, thence it was to proceed to Radstadt, and thereafter to the remaining hamlets of the province. To prevent the secret return of banished persons, their old homes were to be searched at intervals of two weeks. Residents of communities through which refugees were driven were admonished not to employ or shelter anyone, whether married or single, manservant, or maidservant, craftsman or apprentice, old or young.

By November 26, the final date set for the banishment of the first contingent, the movement had got under way in Werfen, Golddeg, and St. Veit. The absence of a well organized plan caused considerable confusion: troops marched hither and yon; and the officers were overburdened with routine reports, inspections, and the necessary quartering of the refugees. Furthermore, the weather was miserable, the roads were bad and almost impassable, and the clogging administrative machinery came to an abrupt halt. More difficulties arose due to the fact that by December 3, passes for seven hundred persons had been processed, in spite of the order of November 26 that only two hundred were to be sent across the border at a time. To aggravate the situation, two thirds of those scheduled to leave were found to be holders of property. Therefore for them a further delay was necessary to enable civil and spiritual officers to extract from them "a pound of flesh": to wit, cash payments for old and forgotten taxes, fees, and feudal dues. In numerous cases, persons who had already been evicted from their homes were detained until the spring of 1732. Persons in some villages, however, ignored the ordered delay.

The procession of refugees, when joined by those rounded up in parts of the Pongau, took on the appearance of a martial band led by military guards. While on the march many of the "Christian soldiers" burst forth in Luther's battle song of the Reformation, "A Mighty Fortress Is Our God," Scheitberger's song of the exiles,

100

"I Am But a Poor Exile," and other songs expressive of their plight and spiritual mood. Among others of the refugees pandemonium was so great as to make it necessary for the army officers in charge to fire above the heads of the marchers and throw dud grenades into their ranks to bring about a semblance of order. Still other persons gladly responded to instructions and joined the march, expecting some of the Protestant princes of Germany, Prussia, and Saxony in particular, to come to their support and help them expel the Catholic peasantry of Salzburg. The Taxbergers looked to the Archduke of Saxony and almost to a man expected to be permitted to remain, or soon to return as conquerors. At Radstadt many a resentful peasant turned loose and drove away his stock.

One Captain Lapponi and his men, who marched forty-eight day laborers via Wagrin to Radstadt, were followed by peasants of Wagrin. These, when they reached the market place, asked for official permission to travel along with the forty-eight. When threatened, they declared that as long as Christ their Savior was their refuge, they feared neither martyrdom nor death. At Radstadt a similar scene was enacted. Poorly clad men, women, and children emerged from their homes, and on bended knees pleaded with the soldiers to be permitted to join the crusade, as they were confident God would not forsake them. Along the line of march from city to city into northern Germany the less informed were indoctrinated with Lutheranism.

The mass expulsion of the Lutheran workers in the salt mines of the Duerrnberg at Hallein posed a serious financial threat to Firmian, for the income from the salt industry was his most lucrative source of revenue. Of the three hundred employees in this enterprise only thirty were Catholic. To have proceeded there as elsewhere would have had serious consequences for him. Sensing his dilemma, the miners were inclined to hold more tenaciously to the Augsburg Confession. It was even rumored that they intended to sabotage the salt works, should they be persecuted on account of religion.

Firmian did whatever was possible to prevent all contacts of the salt workers of the Duerrnberg, whom he wished to bring back to the Catholic fold, with the Pongau refugees. The refugees were routed to bypass the regular route through Hallein on their way to Radstadt and thence to the frontier. This, however, was not entirely successful, for on fair days some met with the Halleiners in the outdoors, and in inclement weather they secretly met in homes and inns. Efforts of missionaries to bring the miners and their families back into the Catholic church failed. Sermons and catechetical instruction in homes went for naught. Frequently when a miner's cabin door was opened to a prying Catholic missionary the family greeted him by singing a Lutheran hymn.

Archbishop Firmian delayed the expulsion of the Hallein salt workers until November 30, 1732 after he had succeeded in recruiting men from Italy and Berchtesgaden to fill their places in the mines. At the border of Bavaria they were delayed in leaving Salzburg until the Dutch government, who wanted them as colonists, assumed all of their financial responsibility from the time they left until their arrival in Holland. Here they were guaranteed freedom of worship and to engage in any occupation which would afford them a living.

Though severely shocked by the loss of so many of his common laborers who chose exile rather than to renounce their faith, Archbishop Firmian expected a lesser percentage of the owners of land to leave. He knew that they would be deeply concerned over the serious decline of land values which would result from the need of liquidating what property they could within three or four months. This was made more difficult by having to sell to Catholics only. Should they fail to sell, only a Catholic could act as agent or administrator. Further to discourage them from leaving, they were told that before they would be permitted to depart, they would have to obtain a special passport and church taxes would have to be paid. In addition, if they chose to leave, obsolete feudal dues and services would be revived and they would be obliged to pay their cash equivalent. As the time of departure drew near they were forewarned of the dangers they would encounter on their way as well as in the land where they might settle. But thousands who were bound for East Prussia were not particularly impressed either by the stories about the danger of bears and wolf-packs in that barren land or by the warning that in East Prussia they would receive less consideration than dogs. In spite of all attempts to discourage them, when the day of the exodus arrived, one band after another marched to the deportation center. To the amazement of the Salzburg administrators, the province of Salzburg lost most

The Drive into the Mountain (Courtesy of Sepp Rostra, Salzburg)

Sara Kantlin of Durnberg

Maria Steinbacherin of Merssen

Hans Klammer, of Bischoffshofen

Ursula Filtzin aus St. Johannis.

Luteri Catechi. muiſ

Der Catechiſmus tan die kleine Bibel heiſsen
und uns den rechten Weg zum Wahren Leben weiſen,
weil ich die Warheit nun aus ſolchen hiberlandt
verlaſse ich getroſt darob mein Vatterland.

Ursula Viltzin, of St. John's

Johann Friedrich Ehrlich, of St. John's

Hanns Kamel, Master of the Salt Works in the Durmberg, Salzburg

Entry from the Salzburg Friedenhall into the City

This reproduction of a picture in the Kaiserhof Hotel in Salzburg shows the procession arranged by the Archbishop and Priests of Salzburg. From left to right: Guild of Mechanics; lay brothers; cathedral clergy; canons; monks of St. Peter; abbots and prelates; bishops; provincial knights; turmpeters; honorary chaplain; the Archbishop; choir *aulaci*; nobles and cavalry.

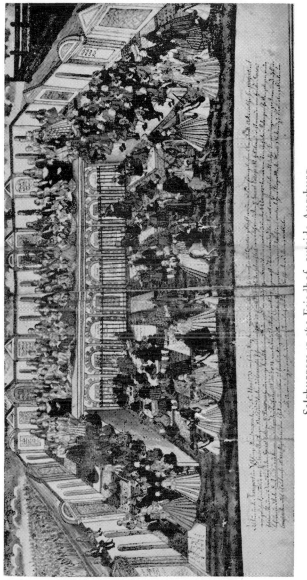

Salzburgers in the Friedhof, outside Augsburg
(Courtesy of the Augsburg Lutheran Deaconate)

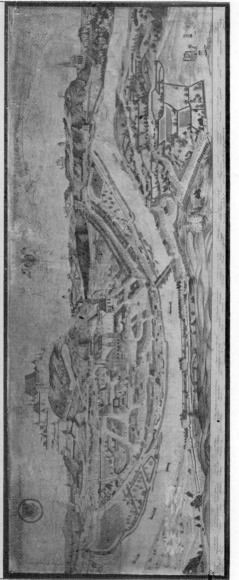

The City of Salzburg, 1553
(Reproduction of picture in Kaiserhof Hotel, Salzburg)

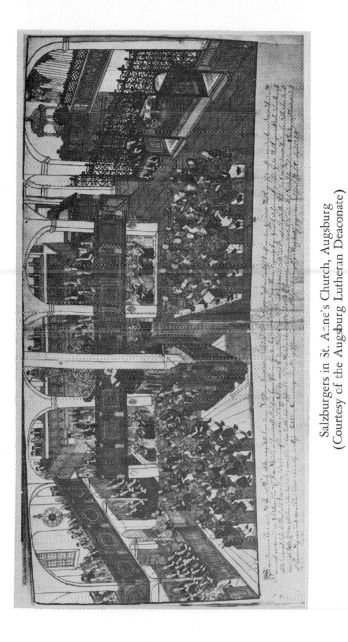

Salzburgers in St. Anne's Church, Augsburg
(Courtesy of the Augsburg Lutheran Deaconate)

Salzburgers in the Schieszgraben, outside Augsburg
(Courtesy of the Augsburg Lutheran Deaconate)

of its enterprising peasants. In the village of St. John alone only fourteen of the families remained.

Between November 1731 and April 1732, the government of Salzburg made an appraisal of all lands owned by the professed Lutherans who were destined for expulsion in the spring. No appeal from the findings of the assessors was permitted. Not until shortly before leaving were those who had failed to dispose of their real estate told the appraised value of their land either in writing or in an oral statement. For some undisclosed reason the major property holder received only an oral statement of the value of his land. Amid the excitement and confusion immediatly preceding the departure many forgot the property valuation given them and lost contact with possible witnesses to the statement of the appraisers. In a final effort to discourage the exodus of some individuals and provoke a return to Catholicism, the government agents were ordered to give each client a glowing description of the beauty and grandeur of Salzburg and of the happy and prosperous life that each had been privileged to enjoy in the home land.

In the interim between the expulsion of the bands of emigrants in the winter of 1731 to '32 and the time set for departure of the propertied class and others they held to their regular occupations. With the approach of spring, many prepared the soil and put in the customary crops. Was it perhaps with a hope that they might be detained longer to help with the harvest? In spite of this they were notified on April 16 that within eight days they would have to leave their homes. Many must have been saddened by memories of the happy past. For as they lifted their eyes upward, they saw the mountains still capped with snow, their verdant slopes watered by the melting snow and studded with flowers in all their spring beauty.

At Saalfeld, Werfen, and Radstadt, herdsmen, shepherds, milkmaids, women and children could not think of forgoing a last opportunity to participate in the customary spring festival. At the appointed time they gathered for the first spring march into the uplands. Before marching they decorated their cattle with gayly flowered garlands and bright peacock foliage and from the brightly embroidered bands which held the wreaths together they suspended Alpine bells. The procession was then formed, and the young women and men, clad in gayly colored garb, took the lead into the upland pasturage. These were followed by the shepherd with his spring flute, and after him the decorated cattle and the milkers with pails and milk containers.

In the gradual ascent the melodious voices of the men, women and children reverberated through the valley as they sang their spring songs. Throughout the day, as they wended their way into the upper reaches of the pasture lands, the muffled melodies drifted downward into the valleys. In anticipation of what was to come, many a silent prayer must have risen to the throne of the Almighty. As the mountains commenced to cast their shadows over the peaceful villages below, the procession slowly descended into the valley from which they were to be ejected the following morning.

Those ordered to drive the Lutheran occupants from hearth and home cared little about seeing that families were kept together. In the rush and confusion, many families in predominantly Lutheran communities like Werfen were separated, not to be united again until they were on their way or in some far-off land. Not the slightest consideration was accorded non-Catholic couples who lived together because they were denied the right of marriage. Sadly enough, their children were, therefore, illegitimate according to the laws of Salzburg. Upon reaching the extradition center, children born outside wedlock were taken from their parents by order of Archbishop Firmian, to be reared in Catholic monasteries. All children over twelve years of age who had remained loyal to the Catholic church were detained and the property of their parents was confiscated by the state supposedly for their support.

The expulsion procedure, in its early stages, lacked adequate preparation and organization. At the beginning Firmian assumed that his neighbors would readily consent to through passage. Before the time set for extradition, hundreds of Lutherans had already gathered along the frontier of Salzburg. On November 24, 1731, nine hundred were concentrated at Wagrin, and could proceed no farther. At the same time eight hundred assembled at Tittmonig near the Bavarian border, and to these were added the hundred and fifty who had been turned away by the Tyrolese government at Innsbruck. Most of these people were poor, and places of shelter for them from the winter cold were entirely inadequate.

Before the Archduke of Bavaria would honor Salzburg passports, the payment of all expense which might be incurred in the march through Bavaria had to be guaranteed. From the small amount given most of the poor by the government of Salzburg each person was obliged to pay the Bavarian agent who supervised the journey through that state. Both Bavaria and Tyrol resented the idea of having persons purported to be "beggars and criminals" enter their territory. They were as much dreaded as foreign soldiers who left in their wake famine and pestilence. To counteract this fear, Cristani reversed his previous statement by declaring that these people passing through were as gentle as lambs. He also wanted to assure passage and to reduce the number of guards that would be demanded by Bavaria.

Little consideration was accorded the first contingent passing through Bavaria to Swabia, where both Protestant and Catholic were tolerated. In spite of being warned against it, many of the populace of Bavaria, almost exclusively Catholic, called the bedraggled wanderers "damned heretics." To this the wanderers responded much as was done in the city of Salzburg under similar circumstances. "Only he who can create has the power to damn." Those later permitted to travel with Salzburg guides to Swabia by way of Switzerland were met by the city officials on Christmas Day when they neared the Swiss town of Wilheim. They entered the town in wretched condition, caused by exposure to deep snow and frost followed by a downpour of rain. On the evening before the last of them had arrived at Wilheim only sixteen Kreuzer were left to purchase food for an average of seventeen persons. From Wilheim they were directed to Schoengau at the Swabian border. Here the Salzburg guide left, taking with him the refugee register, an action which proved particularly annoying to those who had come from Salzburg without passports.

The Protestants of Berchtesgaden could hardly be expected to escape the impact of what was going on in Salzburg. This diminutive principality of eighteen thousand was then governed by Abbot Cajetan Anthon, Freiherr von Nottaffel, and in some respects it rivaled and excelled Salzburg in scenic beauty and Alpine grandeur. Along the lower reaches of its lofty mountains were found the homes and lands of peasant proprietors, while higher up nestled the herdsmen's and cheesemakers' homes, locally dubbed *Kaese* (cheese).

For generations intimate contacts had existed between the salt workers of the Duerrnberg at Hallein and those at Berchtesgaden. The Protestants of this small mountain community, once the expulsion of the Lutherans at Salzburg was well under way, asked leave of Cajetan Anton to follow them into exile. Rather than voice serious objections to the request, he did what he could to discourage emigration. For example, well-to-do peasants were required to pay the government ten Gulden before they were permitted to leave and the poorer had to pay five. In addition, as in Salzburg, they were ordered to make cash payments fixed by the abbot in lieu of long-forgotten feudal dues and services. And further, beginning at the time of the request, they were denied the benefit of clergy and the right of a Christian burial.

Of greatest concern to Anton was the possible loss of a host of highly skilled workers. For nearly every home in Berchtesgaden was a small factory with all but the very young having a part in the fashioning of some specific article. Woodcarvings of every description were expertly made in most of the homes and sold in foreign markets. These articles were purchased by the international merchants from Augsburg and Nuernberg. To prevent competitive industries from springing up in these export centers, the heads of families who chose to leave Berchtesgaden were bound by an oath not to settle in either of the two cities.

The people of Salzburg and Berchtesgaden were by nature a hardy, industrious, and liberty-loving folk. Throughout the crisis in Salzburg in the second quarter of the eighteenth century, hostility toward the authoritarian trend associated with the concept of the sovereign state was quite apparent. This was to be expected in a localized daily environment where "do it yourself" had to be a way of life. The Salzburgers, to a lesser extent than their Berchtesgaden neighbors, specialized in household industries: by nature and necessity they were carpenters, cabinet makers, and masons. The farmer, in particular, had an important part in building and enlarging his home and constructing the facilities so important in a farming community. He and his neighbors were skilled as wagon builders, wheelwrights, and makers of tools for tilling the soil. Many tanned and prepared leather, which they furnished the itinerant cobbler, who went from house to house to make and repair shoes. Salzburg, blessed with more and better lands than Berchtesgaden, was known to have efficient and frugal farmers and herdsmen. Nearly every master cattleman owned from fifty to a hundred head of cattle, fifty sheep, and at least three goats for breeding purposes. Is it any wonder that states of northern Europe, even

Russia, bid against each other and agreed to finance the journey and the settlement of these thrifty folks in their country?

In the early stage of this movement, whereby Salzburg lost at least one seventh of its total population in less than a decade, the outside world obtained little reliable information, for Archbishop Firmian clamped as tight a censorship as possible upon the happenings in the archbishopric. Whether or not Salzburg was engaged in putting down a rebellion with the aid of foreign troops, as was rumored, was not known. The first account of what was happening was that given by a calvary officer of Prince Eugene's command. On his arrival at Ratisbon from Salzburg, he reported to the Bavarian legate of the German Diet that all was calm in Salzburg. He affirmed that the Lutherans had peaceably surrendered their arms and all their physical means of defense. At the same time a Prussian representative in the Diet pointed out the absurdity of the report that Salzburg was in the throes of a rebellion. To him it did not make sense to think that a mere handful of imperial soldiers could put down an uprising of twenty to thirty thousand mountain folk who yere thoroughly familiar with the rugged terrain of Salzburg. On the other hand, in the Diet the representative of Salzburg claimed that Firmian was obliged to rid himself of these rebels as quickly as possible because of the expense of maintaining foreign troops in his prince-archbishopric.

CHAPTER XIII

PROTESTANT PRINCES INTERCEDE

ARCHBISHOP FIRMIAN was successful in confronting the Holy Roman Emperor, Charles VI, and the German princes with a *fait accompli,* but was only partly successful in censoring news out of Salzburg until the exodus was well under way. Hardly had the systematic eviction of Lutherans started when reports of it filtered out to the European chancelleries. Even before the Bavarian border had been opened to the refugees from Salzburg, the Emperor, undoubtedly in response to pressure from the Protestant princes, filed a formal protest against Firmian's *Emigrationspatent.*

However, Charles VI could ill afford to antagonize either Firmian or the Protestant princes of the Diet, for the fate of the Pragmatic Sanction, on the Diet agenda for consideration in January, 1733, hung in the balance. But, to placate the princes, Charles called on the archbishop to abide by Article V of the Treaty of Westphalia, which granted banished persons three years in which to liquidate their assets. At the same time, he called for a more humane approach to the decree of expulsion.

The response to the Emperor's criticism and demands was bold and without precedent in the history of eighteenth-century diplomacy. Cristani, Firmian's secretary, made much of the Archbishop's loyalty to Charles VI. He took the Emperor to task for his reprimand, and reminded him that on no previous occasion had he protested when other German princes had adopted a like policy. To Cristani such action on the part of the Emperor seemed poor thanks for Firmian's steadfast support. The Salzburg officials, however, must have been aware that Charles could hardly have ignored an act which banished so large a number of persons from hearth and home in so short a time and regardless of the approach of winter.

Since the Reformation, banishment from one's homeland for refusing to conform to the Catholic faith had been very common. However, after the adoption of the Religious Peace of Augsburg

(1555), religion was made a matter of territorial rather than of personal concern. Each prince of the Empire could decide whether his subjects were to adhere to Lutheranism or to Catholicism, Which of these two was to prevail within any principality rested entirely with the territorial prince. Almost a century later the Treaty of Westphalia, which concluded the Thirty Years' War, contained a similar privilege for Calvinist princes.

The Emperor was fully aware of Firmian's influence in the Diet as presiding officer of the House of Lords. Not only might he block the acceptance of the Pragmatic Sanction by some of the princes of the Empire, but he might ally himself with the archdukes of Bavaria and of the Palatinate, who opposed the act. To prevent this, Charles VI sent his vice chancellor and personal envoy, Franz Gentilotti, to negotiate with Firmian.

It was at this juncture that Gentilotti and Firmian's secretary, Cristani, schemed to have the Archbishop absolved of all responsibility for the sudden exodus of Lutherans from Salzburg. The two planned to trick the peasants themselves into relinquishing all rights guaranteed by the Treaty of Westphalia. Local officials were secretly instructed to frame a petition and then have the peasants concerned sign it. After its content had been explained, each peasant was to be asked to sign it. Signatures of persons who could not write were to be attested to by the enrolling officers. Needless to say, comparatively few persons acted voluntarily. The whole procedure was clothed in utmost secrecy. At all odds, Italian and Imperial officers were to be kept in ignorance of what was going on.

In the petition the peasants stated that they regretted that religious services had been prohibited outside the home, and they humbly begged Firmian to forgive and forget their infractions against his orders. He was asked to show clemency and release the convicted Protestants from the prison and permit these to depart with them on the later date of April 24, (1732).

Forthwith, on February 29, the Archbishop had the peasants' request forwarded to Vienna and he publicly announced that they had voluntarily absolved themselves of every consideration set forth in the Treaty of Westphalia. Furthermore, he announced that ten prisoners had been released, and he gave the assurance that those remaining would be accorded every consideration. Permission was granted for those departing to leave on April 24 and all local agents then were ordered to hasten their expulsion. At a request from Vienna, the remaining prisoners were released without a formal trial, but in their passports they were classified as criminals. Thereafter, Emperor Charles VI was little concerned over what the Protestant princes thought or said.

In September of the same year (1732) word reached the Archbishop that the Emperor was contemplating a visit to Linz on the Danube. Thereupon, Firmian made elaborate preparations for a personal visit with Charles. He picked 82 retainers to precede him and to make all necessary arrangements for the formal reception at the Castle Hagen near Linz. The party traveled down the Inn River to where it enters the Danube at Inns, and thence up the Danube a distance of nine miles to the city of Lintz.

They traveled in three large boats and took with them three coaches and eighteen magnificent horses to draw the coaches. The party was supplied with every culinary need for kitchen, pastry shop, and wine cellar. Firmian, before his return to Salzburg, dropped in on the chamberlain of the Castle Hagen, the temporary residence of Firmian, and presented him with a set of knives with gold handles valued at 600 Florins.[1] To the chief butler he gave a dozen each of spoons, knives and forks set in exquisite porcelain and valued at 500 Florins. The lord high steward and each of the pages received 25 ducats. For the lord of the castle, Firmian had 1,000 Florins. Incidentally, Firmian, who hunted by the side of the Emperor, had the happy fortune of bagging a deer.

Preceding the time set for dining with the imperial couple and their guests, at the castle in Linz, Firmian besought the lord high chancellor to intercede for him with the Emperor, to have him elevated to the rank of archduke. Then, before the guests were to be seated at the table, Firmian had himself posted at a place where he could not be seen but from which he had a view of the dining table. After noting where the royal couple were seated, he arranged to have himself seated in an armchair to the right of Charles VI. He also saw to it that he was brought in over a red carpet, intended only for royalty, instead of a green one. The ensuing conversation between the Emperor and Firmian was concerned almost exclusively with the *Emigrationspatent* and its consequences.

---

[1] J. Dye, *Coin Encyclopedia* (1887), estimates the value of a florin at $1.75 and of a ducat at $2.30. Today the purchasing power would be far greater.

In the course of their conversation they agreed upon a more moderate policy toward the Lutherans who still remained in Salzburg. The agreement was wordy, and full of loopholes, and was of little consequence because few Lutherans then remained in Salzburg. Between November 24, 1731, and September 1732, approximately 20,000 Lutherans had departed. Fewer than 7,000 were still to be accounted for. On March 20, 1733, 900 from Berchtesgaden were on their way out. In the years following the settlement of a band of refugees in Hungary in 1734, Lutheran departures from Salzburg trickled on for more than a decade.

To minimize the adverse criticism by the Protestant princes of Germany, Firmian sought to add fuel to the fire of the religious feud which existed then between Calvinists and Lutherans. In a published protocol he tried to prove that the peasants concerned should be prosecuted as disturbers of the peace. He asserted that a majority of them subscribed to doctrines which bore no semblance to those taught by Luther or Calvin. Therefore, they could not lay claim to consideration as granted in Article IV of the Treaty of Westphalia. It was emphasized that since Salzburg had no part in the Thirty Years' War and had not signed the peace treaty it was not bound by the terms of Westphalia. Furthermore, when Archbishop Max Gandolf of Salzburg banished non-Catholics in 1685—the Emperor had taken similar action a few years earlier—neither Lutheran nor Calvinist had protested.

Firmian's accusations, instead of sharpening the cleavage between the two denominations, had an opposite effect. For the first time since the Reformation, Lutherans and Calvinists forgot their differences and rallied to the defense of the Protestant Salzburgers. They reproved the Archbishop and called on him to adopt a policy of moderation in harmony with the Westphalian Pact. Much was expected of the King of Prussia, at that time the most powerful and influential Protestant prince of Germany. Even rulers outside the Empire threatened to retaliate against their Catholic constituents, in a vain hope that the pontiff would raise his voice against Firmian's ruthless procedure. The kings of Denmark and of Sweden demanded that the Archbishop either rescind or temper his order. In case he failed to do so, each threatened to retaliate against his Catholic subjects. The King of Sweden, a guarantor of the treaty which ended the Thirty Years' War, promised to do what he could on behalf of his religious brethren in Salzburg. If his appeal were ignored, he would sever diplomatic relations with Salzburg. Holland, a country of religious toleration, proceeded to impose religious restrictions upon the freedom of Catholic worship in the home. In particular that was to be the case in the Catholic territory which had been ceded to Holland in 1648.

Unfortunately, the international situation was such that the oral and written threats by the Protestant princes could be ignored with abandon by the government of Salzburg. Only Frederick William I of Prussia (1713-1740) seemed ready to proceed along constructive lines, and then only when circumstances at home seemed opportune. He was then preoccupied with Prussian reconstruction and administrative reorganization after the War of the Spanish succession (1701-1713), and these matters engaged his attention until the spring of 1732. He was also much concerned with other difficulties and dangers, some national and some personal. For several years, from 1726 on, East Prussia was ravaged by a deadly plague which wiped out much of its population. On July 1, 1730, Frederick William I abruptly terminated the dynastic marriage negotiations between the royal houses of Prussia and England. A month later Prince Frederick, heir to the Prussian throne, and his intimate companion, Katte, were apprehended at the Prussian border on the way to England where they hoped to escape the Spartan discipline of the eccentric Frederick William I. The latter had said of his son Fritz, *"Er ist ein effemineter Kerl"* (he is an effeminate fellow). The father of Fritz had no sympathy with his son's love for French poetry and his interest in the trends of the eighteenth century enlightenment. The two companions were imprisoned in the royal castle, were tried, found guilty of treason, and sentenced to be executed. Katte was executed in the courtyard in full view of Frederick's prison window and his body allowed to remain there to make sure Fritz would see it. For days a father confessor was sent to visit the royal prisoner, Prince Frederick, but not until August 1731 was a reconciliation between father and son effected.

In the same year external affairs took on a menacing aspect. From the first quarter of 1731 to March 16, 1732, an ominous war cloud, which threatened to engulf the major powers, hung over all of Europe. Not until an Anglo-Austrian alliance had been negotiated was the tension in Europe eased sufficiently to enable the Prussian king to act on behalf of the Salzburgers.

Once Frederick William I had convinced himself of the uprightness and the industry of the Salzburgers he began to show particular interest in them. Among the first of his acts was to appeal to the Catholic leaders of Germany and to the Pope that they intercede with Firmian for the adoption of a more humane policy. The Prussian sovereign threatened to impose religious restrictions on the Catholic cities of Magdeburg, Minden, and Halberstadt, annexed to Prussia in 1648. At a conclave of Minden priests called by Frederick William I, he told the Catholic clergy that he would retaliate against the Catholics, should Firmian fail to adopt a less severe policy of expulsion. In such an event the Catholic churches of Minden would be closed and their property would be confiscated, something which never happened.

To ease the tension and assure the Salzburgers of a haven of refuge, Schenkendorf, Emperor Charles VI's personal representative at Ratisbon, assured Frederick William I that the refugees from Salzburg would be a valuable asset to Prussia. With that in mind, the King of Prussia in April, 1732, expressed a willingness to accept a thousand of them. This was followed in June of the same year by a bid for ten thousand, and in the following month by a promise to facilitate and finance the settlement of as many in Prussia as would care to come. Tradesmen, laborers, peasants, and cattlemen were welcomed and assured of generous consideration. They were guaranteed royal protection and freedom of worship, no matter what their faith.

To get the movement under way, a Prussian officer with the necessary funds was sent to Ratisbon. Each man who would agree to settle in Prussia received for his own use four Groschen per day, each woman three, and each child two. Assurance was also given by the Prussian representative that his government would assist in the liquidation of the property of all who had been unable to attend to such things before leaving Salzburg.

According to the decree of the Prussian representative, all who chose to emigrate to his country were assured of all rights, privileges and immunities accorded Prussian citizens. In addition, masters and all others plying a specific trade were to be granted the same consideration as persons of a similar craft in Prussia. They were permitted to take up residence and practice their art in whatever city they might choose. Upon taking an oath of citizenship and establishing their status as craftsmen they would be exempt from all taxes and dues for one year. Persons skilled in cloth making, particularly serge, flannel, and shoddy, and in the fashioning of hats, who were willing to practice their craft at an assigned locality, would be given a three-year tax holiday. Anyone willing to take up residence in an agricultural area which had been laid waste by war or denuded of its population by disease would receive not only the land he was able to cultivate but also, without cost to him, all material necessary for building a home and other facilities. Whoever went to Prussia at his own expense was guaranteed a ten-year tax exemption. Those who wished to establish a group settlement were privileged to do so. Such a settlement would be surveyed and plotted at no expense to them and should be named for Salzburg.

Princes and administrative officers of states through which these Prussian immigrants found it necessary to travel were requested to assure them of free and safe conduct. Frederick William I readily agreed to the payment of all their expenses including those for food and lodging. At Nuernberg in the course of their trek 20,694 immigrants were received by the Prussian commissioner; of these 13,944 arrived at Koenigsberg. However, only 12,901 were still alive in 1734, because of the mortality rate among the aged and children who found it difficult to adjust themselves to the food and climate of East Prussia. While on the way some of the refugees, at the point of exhaustion, refused to continue and settled in communities through which they marched. Wherever they settled in considerable numbers, Frederick William I saw to the building of schools and churches for them.

Dutch representatives traveled through the cities of Germany to invite Salzburgers to settle in Holland. They assured the refugees religious freedom, payment of travel expenses, the privilege of settling where they might choose. A similar offer was made in particular to the refugees from Berchtesgaden by the King of England. He was particularly desirous of having them as settlers in his kingdom of Hanover. He was above all impressed by their skill as weavers, especially of linen, spinners of wool, tailors, wheelwrights, carpenters, shoemakers, farmers, day laborers, woodcutters, and tobacco planters. Sweden expressed a desire for miners and ironworkers.

The initial confusion incident to the expulsion of the Protestants from Salzburg soon gave way to an orderly and ably managed exodus. Competent persons were employed to organize and direct

114

emigrant groups. If at all possible, and barring unnecessary delays, the periods of departure were so spaced as to prevent too many persons from moving in on a city at one time. Thus more adequate facilities could be provided for them. Had it not been for the rallying of Protestant Europe to the cause of the Salzburgers, casualties among the wanderers would have been appalling.

In the first year of the exodus, funds sent to a central treasury at Ratisbon were in the amount of 836,863 Florins.[2] England contributed 228,224, Holland 401,928, the Jews of Hamburg 20,091, and the city itself 28,441, Nuernberg 10,354, Hanover 90,000, and Denmark 57,827. Other collecting agencies were located at Koenigsberg and Augsburg, while many other cities acted independently of these. Contributions from all Protestant countries of Europe continued to flow into strategic Protestant centers through which the refugees passed. Cities, towns, villages, and hamlets rose to the occasion, and even Catholic communities were caught in the tide. In places where they were obliged to stop one or more nights the value of gifts in the form of money, food, clothing, and other necessities must have exceeded the total amount deposited to their account at Ratisbon and other depositories.

By 1733, twenty-three well-organized Lutheran groups had taken leave of Salzburg. These ranged from 109 to approximately 1000 persons. One of the largest of these groups was the eighth, which at first consisted of 864 persons. On May 6, 1732, they left via Schoengau and arrived in Augsburg on May 18. Upon leaving Augsburg, their number had increased to 930 and at Schoenburg another 100 joined them. Of the total number, 40 had been charged in Salzburg with disturbing the peace, and 30 claimed they had been imprisoned in the dungeon of the fortress of Hohensalzburg. Some were very well-to-do and had to leave behind property valued as upward of 15,000 Taler.[3] From 1733 to 1740, fairly small contingents of refugees left Salzburg.

Perhaps one of the most, if not the most, affluent company of 419 set out from Salzburg in August 1732. Unlike the others, none traveled on foot. The procession was made up of several carts and 38 wagons, eight of which were freight transports. Fifteen of these conveyances hauled women and children; three coaches carried the

---

[2]Hans Widmann, *Geschichte Salzburg*, VIII, p. 417. £ = approximately 6½ florins at that time.
[3]*Ibid.*, p. 417. £ = approximately 4 Taler.

wives of the prominent members of the company; and one contained a lone mother and her three children. Property left behind by one member of this group, an inn keeper, was assessed at 22,000 Taler, that of a farmer at 20,000 Taler and that of the least well-to-do person at 1,000 Taler.

Quite likely emigrant letters which got through to relatives tended to persuade others to leave. A letter of a settler in Prussia to a brother-in-law in Salzburg said that they lacked nothing on their way, and that wherever they stopped they were kindly received. In fact, he continued, they were so well treated that they forgot what had happened to them. In a letter to his son, a father in Prussia described his building a new home for which the king furnished all material free of cost. In addition, the family was supplied with all necessities until a time when it could be self-supporting.

CHAPTER XIV

PROTESTANT EUROPE UNITES

THE EXODUS of the Salzburgers had hardly begun when all of Protestant Europe seemed to rise to the occasion. Almost overnight all of Europe was flooded with a mass of literature extolling their virtues. Old and young alike were praised as martyrs who were ready to take leave of their beloved and enchanted homeland and brave wind and weather for the sake of their faith. A contemporary pamphleteer aptly remarked: "It seems as if 20,000 times the number of those who were exiled were on the move. The countenance of each and every one of them radiated the glow of religious ecstasy and a childlike faith,"[1] Wherever they traveled the old and familiar folk songs seemed to take on new meaning, and Luther's battle song of the Reformation, *Ein Feste Burg ist unser Gott* (A Mighty Fortress Is Our God), Scheitberger's *Song of an Exile,* and many other spiritual anthems sung by the Salzburgers added fuel to the embers of a waning Protestantism. Medals and coins were struck commemorating the occasion, and about a half century later, the poet Goethe memorialized one of the scenes from the trek in his *Hermann und Dorothea.*

Never since the Reformation had anything like this happened to put an end to factional bickering within Protestant ranks and to unite them for a common cause. The spontaneous and enthusiastic religious revival amazed and confounded Catholic Europe. Words of sympathy and admiration for the spiritual fortitude of the Salzburgers were matched by liberal contributions collected in all parts of Europe. Money, clothing, household linens, household necessities, Bibles, hymnals, and religious tracts were showered on the refugees as they traveled from place to place. Relief agencies through which funds were gathered for them were established in Ratisbon, Dresden, Augsburg, and other German centers. Even

[1]Quoted in C. Fr. Arnold, *Die Ausrottung des Protestantismus in Salzburg,* p. 13.

117

English merchants in Asia Minor and Venice rendered financial assistance.

Volk, in a description of the reception of the Salzburgers wrote:[2]

> Rumors of the departure of the first detachments of the Salzburgers soon spread like wildfire. All of German Protestantism was overcome with an enthusiasm and its contagion extended into Jewish and Catholic ranks. It almost seemed, when troop after troop was driven from its home in the spring of 1732, that Firmian had made up his mind to rid the valleys of his principality of their population. The refugees in their march to Berlin reminded one of the flight of Israelites from Egypt into the Promised Land. The charitable contributions heaped upon them as they traveled from place to place seemed to be without limit. As they entered town after town, they were embraced by the populace as if they were long-lost friends. Amid shouts of joy they were invited into homes where they were greeted by the enticing odor of food which awaited them. When the time of departure arrived, their host came to tears and acted as though one of his own was being torn from him.
>
> Distrust of them suddenly gave way to an emotional enthusiasm for the martyrs from Salzburg. Small children who had nothing to offer shared their *Butterbemme* (bread and butter) for breakfast with the strangers. In many of the cities, persons of rank entertained them and they themselves performed all menial services.
>
> On Maundy Thursday, much after the manner of the "Holy Father" and the higher Catholic clergy, prominent persons of the community washed the feet of the poor elder Salzburgers and when they departed they showered them with presents. The renowned theologian, Dr. Georg Ludwig Boemer, proudly told in later years when he was at Goettingen that he and other Halle professors considered it an honor to serve the Salzburg martyrs while they were dining. The Count of Koburg, his mother, wife, brother, and two princesses considered it a favor to set before them plates filled with food and to remove the empty dishes when their honored

[2]W. Volk, *Die Auswanderung der protestantisch gesinnten Salzburger in den Jahren* 1731-1372, p. 495.

guests had dined. City councilmen and knights served food and drink for them and waited until the Salzburgers had finished before they sat down to eat. Not only were their hosts deeply moved by the misfortune which had come to the Salzburgers, but even the most hardened souls were rendered speechless by the sight of them.

Volk, himself an ardent Catholic, said:[3]

Wherever they went they were likened to the early Christian martyrs. This tended to turn their heads, gave them a martyr-complex, and filled them with a passionate desire to measure up to such a criterion. All Germany was overcome by an epidemic of adulation for these Salzburg saints. Even Jews and Catholics were carried away by the enthusiastic reception accorded to them. Servants at Erfurt thought it an honor and a privilege to give to them of their meager personal wardrobe.

In the Tyrol everything possible was done to dull the impact of the movement. Even Catholic Italy was caught in the tidal wave of this religious revival which threatened to engulf all of Christendom.

The contemporary historian, Schelhorn, deeply moved by the memorable exodus which he ascribed to Divine guidance, wrote:[4]

God had in his infinite wisdom foreordained the movement and revealed it in all its splendor through the Salzburgers. This epochal event in our time transcends all others which have manifested themselves throughout the centuries of history. In the Salzburg exodus one can envisage a living image of the flight of the Children of Israel from Egypt. Old men with ice-gray hair, men stooped and trembling from age, walked resolutely along with young men in the prime of life. Feeble and elderly women kept pace with spry maidens and youthful and handsome girls. To all of these God had

---

[3]Volk, *op. cit.*, p. 548.

[4]Quoted in Arnold, pp. 79-81; Johannes G. Schelhorn *Historische Nachricht von Ursprunge, Fortgang, er. Schicksale der Evang. Religion in den Salzburgischen Landen,* p. 408.

spoken as to our spiritual Father Abraham when he ordered him to leave Ur and said to him: "Get thee out of thy country, and from thy kindred . . . unto a land that I will show you . . . I will bless thee and make thee great."

In a similar strain a contemporary pamphleteer quoted from the Prophet Isaiah: "The Lord God which gathereth the outcasts of Israel saith, yet will I gather others to me, beside those that are gathered unto him."

Still another writer proclaimed:

> What God has done in these days for His church will resound to His glory throughout the Holy Roman Empire. These emigrants who, are destined to wander to all parts of the earth, will be a living symbol to all mankind of the power of His word and the glory of His Holy Spirit. Without the aid of sermons and public processions, God's divine power has manifested itself through the weak.[5]

It goes without saying that in such an atmosphere of spiritual exhilaration miraculous stories would follow in the wake of these chosen servants of the Most High. One of these was told by a pilgrim from Gera:

> Bibles were being burned in Salzburg and a part of a page containing the words "heaven and earth shall pass, but my word endureth forever" was blown from the flames and was picked up and again confined to the fire only to be carried out unscathed by the wind. It was then seized, torn into bits, and trampled under foot.

Another told of a man who was fifty years of age being cast into a filthy dungeon. "For two months he was confined to utter darkness and mired in filth to his armpits, but the Lord permitted him to emerge unharmed." Still another told of a woman who was cast into a fiery furnace and escaped from it without even being singed. A final story told of a band of Salzburgers who in the course of their wandering were miraculously fed with bread which they gathered from trees.[6]

---

[5]Johann A. Walther, Pamphlet bound with Schelhorn, 24 pp.
[6]Walther, *op. cit.*

Pastor Andrew Walther of Gera in Saxony exclaimed in a current pamphlet:

Everywhere, whether in Saxony or any other state or principality of Germany, the miraculous manner with which God works among people in all walks of life was manifested by the Salzburg trek. The news that the Salzburgers were approaching a city suddenly transformed it into a community which seethed with enthusiasm. Folks ran, walked, rode, and went by horseback to meet them. As they walked forth toward and into the city the inspired mass of townsmen who had gone forth to meet them followed them and proceeded on either side of them into the city and through its streets. These were crowded with spectators, doors and windows were thrown open to greet and welcome the noted visitors. Every door seemed to beckon and say to them "enter and find meat, drink, and lodging." Husband, wife, daughter, son, and servant rushed out from home and grasped their hands, drew them close, and said to them, "Come in, you blessed of the Lord, why should you remain outdoors? Come eat and drink to your hearts' content." These Salzburgers, tanned by wind and weather, with beautiful and sparkling eyes, were a sight never to be forgotten. Of one accord the people of the community gladly made contributions for them to the amount of hundreds, yes, thousands of Thalers. One received cloth, another linen, still others shoes, stockings, coats, vests, and bed warmers, all of which were taken from homes and shops. These were carried out to them, thrust into their hands and thrown to them as they passed by in conveyances, and many other gifts were showered upon them with wishes of God's blessing. The Salzburgers, on the other hand, looked upon their hosts and benefactors as guardian angels.

The author then concludes with the words: "Verily, the wondrous work of God was glorified to all who were privileged to see what was being enacted before their eyes."[7]

---

[7]Walther, *op. cit.*

Walther then continues with an account of the entrance of 500 Salzburgers into the city of Gera on April 16, 1732:

A considerable part of the city's inhabitants hastened out to meet them. Outside the city gate they formed two columns, so spaced as to enable the Salzburgers to march between them. As soon as the refugees sighted the Gerans they formed into a column of twos with the men taking the lead, followed by women and children. As the procession moved into the city, all joined in singing "A Mighty Fortress Is Our God," "I Am a Poor Exile," and other hymns appropriate to the occasion. Townsmen broke ranks to lend a helping hand to the aged by grasping their arms and leading them on their way. Children were taken from the arms of their mothers, were kissed and embraced by welcoming townsfolks. After a songfest, prayers, and an address of welcome, they were parceled out in the homes of Gera. On the day following, Thursday, religious services were conducted for the honored guests and, as was wont, when they departed they were given money and personal apparel. That night, however, before they were settled, 250 rain-soaked Salzburgers arrived in the city by wagon. All but twenty of the more robust were conveyed from Gera to a nearby town on their way to Prussia by way of Leipzig. With few exceptions in every community, similar scenes were enacted. At Gotha in Thuringia, when it was reported that Salzburgers were soon due to arrive, the city council ordered a survey made of the city to ascertain how many might be accommodated. Hardly had four streets been canvassed, when the necessary quota was filled.[8]

On July 28, 1732, the city bell of Gotha was rung to announce the approach of the refugees, and it was the signal for the assembling of the town's students, teachers, preachers, councilmen, officials of the ruling prince, and the citizens in preparation for the march to meet the oncoming guests. From the town limits the procession of the multitude of varied citizens from Gotha, followed by the Salzburgers, marched to the market place amid the sound of bells and the singing of anthems. Following a brief address of welcome, the joint recital of the Lord's Prayer, and

---

[8]Walther, *op. cit.*

122

the singing of "Now Thank We All Our God," the refugee guests were taken to their respective quarters. Frederick, Duke of Gotha, entertained 130 of them at his castle, *Friedrichstein*. Before they departed, he gave them a Cordovan leather-bound Weimar Bible. After making an impression of his official seal on the fly leaf of the sacred book, he wrote under the seal: "This Bible is a gift to the poor Salzburgers who have journeyed through Gotha."

Frequently bands of Salzburgers arrived unannounced at the confines of a city. A typical case was that at the imperial city of Kaufbeuern on December 27, 1731. When the watchmen were preparing to close the city gate for the night, 40 strangers made their appearance and requested lodging for themselves and many others who were to arrive some time later. The populace was aghast at the news that an additional 800 was soon to arrive. After dark, the Salzburgers entered the city, followed by five wagons bearing the sick and the children. They were all lodged for the night in Protestant homes. On the following day, in spite of the protest by the four Catholic councilmen, the Mayor of Kaufbeuern had them entertained at public expense. The sick were cared for in the municipal hospital and 63 of the others found employment in the city, some as servants, others as skilled tradesmen such as weavers, cloth shearers, dyers, artistic printers, and makers of braid. Those leaving the next morning split up into three groups, each from neighboring communities in Salzburg. One headed for Memmigen and the others for Kempen and Augsburg.

At Nuernberg when it was announced that voluntary religious exiles from Berchtesgaden were on their way from Ratisbon, elaborate preparations were made for their reception. They were already a popular subject for conversation throughout Germany, and curious spectators from nearby communities joined the city populace who had gathered to welcome them. As the exiles approached, the green hats which the men were swinging in their rhythmic march were first visible.

At Chemnitz in Prussia the first band of refugees was met outside the city by 4000 persons, including the mayor, the council, and the school children. Amid the peal of church bells and the sound of songs, they marched between a double column formed by the 4000.

Perhaps the most trying experience was that braved by the Lutherans who were expelled from Salzburg on November 29, 1732.

Not until February 21, 1733, did they arrive at their journey's end in Holland. Bitter cold weather and heavy snow had made the overland roads impassable and compelled them to travel by water wherever and whenever that was possible. From Salzburg they made their way down the Salzach to the confluence of the river Inn, and down it to where the Inn flows into the Danube at Passau. Their travel up the Danube at Passau was delayed for several days until the ice jams had cleared sufficiently for them to continue on their journey. To tarry in the city, the consent of the Archbishop of Passau was necessary, and not until all arrangements for lodging at the inns of the city had been made were they permitted to enter the city, and then only one at a time. As soon as was humanly possible, they again took to boats to travel up the Danube. Then, after two hazardous days, they were obliged to travel to Ratisbon by wagon at great expense. They reached the city on December 13 and 14, during the bitterest cold spell of the winter.

They were detained at Ratisbon until January 9, 1732, and while there they negotiated with a representative of the Dutch government concerning settlement in Holland. Under the guidance of the Reverend Johann Gottlob Fischer, who had made the necessary arrangements for defraying all of their expenses for travel and entertainment, they set out overland for Wuerzburg by way of Nuernberg, Bavaria. At Wuerzburg, where they embarked to travel down the Main River to the Rhine, the Salzburgers, when passing in their boats under the stone bridge over the Main, were pelted with stones and reviled as "damned heretics" and "descendants of Lucifer" by hoodlums who had gathered on the bridge. After a brief delay at Bonn on the Rhine, they arrived in Cologne on February 11. On the 12th they left Cologne by way of Duesseldorf, and arrived at Nimwegen, Holland on February 21.

The voluntary Lutheran exiles from Berchtesgaden who were permitted to depart for Hanover from their mountain home-land in April, 1733, followed much the same course as that taken by the Salzburgers on the way to Holland, but they were not plagued by inclement weather, and therefore were able to reach their destination, Ratisbon, much more quickly. Archbishop Firmian granted them permission to travel by way of Hallein and from there they journeyed by boat on the Salza and the Inn to Passau and thence up the Danube. However, little concern was shown for them along the way as they traveled from Hallein to their destination. Up the Danube from Passau they successfully negotiated the rapids and crags at Vilshoffen, and for the night they tied their craft a short distance upstream, only to have them cut loose some time later. Fortunately, their boats were not damaged, and they were able to proceed on schedule and to reach Ratisbon on May 2. Here the Berchtesgadeners were accorded the same consideration as the Salzburgers had received. Christian literature and clothing for them which had been channeled from England through Augsburg, Germany, were parceled out among them. While in the city, each of them was accorded the same financial assistance from the Salzburg fund as had been given the refugees from Salzburg.

On May 15 they were again on their way, and on May 28 they reached Frankfurt, and on June 12, four hundred and twenty men, not including the women and children who came with them, arrived in Hanover. Here they were accorded the usual form of reception and were asked to accept money, gifts and clothing in recognition of their contribution to the Evangelical cause in Europe. A total of 150 exiles were settled in other parts of the kingdom. At Hesse-Cassel in anticipation of their arrival a purse of four thousand Thaler had been raised for them.

At this point it seems appropriate to observe that by and large the Catholics were not always inconsiderate of the Protestant refugees. One of the groups, on its way from Memmingen to Bieberach, found that the most covenient line of march was through the free Benedictine principality of Ochsenhausen. Here, the abbot, in response to a request made by the exiles in January, not only granted them free passage through the territory, but also assured them of comfortable lodging, food, and entertainment without cost to them.

On the whole, it would seem that the emigrant bands bound for Prussia encountered more opposition than others. Whether this was because of a larger constituent membership of each of the groups and the greater number of these groups, or because of the ascendant position held by King Frederick William I of Prussia in European affairs is difficult to ascertain. However, a feeling did exist that Frederick William I was quite willing to capitalize on the charitable reaction toward the Salzburgers by routing them through more highly populated areas, rather than have them follow the most direct routes. The first detachment of fifteen hundred, which left Salzburg from Schoengau, arrived at Kauffbeuren on March 22, 1732. Here they were divided into three groups traveling by way of Dortmund, Memmingen, and Oberdorf in the Augsburg diocese. The latter group was barred from the village and was obliged to join the one on the way to Memmingen. Another group, on the way to Nuernberg, when prohibited from entering Bamberg, charged that they were given kindlier treatment by the Jews than by the Catholics of that town.

On the way to Prussia more than 1300 Salzburgers cleared through Nuernberg. Some of the more important cities in Germany through which guided groups traveled were Donauwoerth, Heidelberg, Augsburg, Gera, Halle, Leipzig, Wittenberg, Berlin, and Danzig. At Donauwoerth, a predominantly Catholic city, little difficulty in obtaining proper overnight accommodations for the refugees was encountered by the Prussian officer charged with their supervision. None of the communities, as such, through which the Prussian-bound Salzburgers traveled was put to any expense for them, and any contributions made were matters of voluntary, personal charity. When a band of the exiles came to Christian-Erlang, they found Frenchmen of kindred spirit who received them with open arms. These Protestants, or Huguenots, had been given a haven of refuge here by Frederick William I, when in 1685 Louis XIV wiped out the last vestige of religious toleration by his Revocation of the Edict of Nantes.

The free imperial city of Augsburg, which owed allegiance only to the German emperor, ranked second only to Ratisbon as a clearing center for Salzburgers who were in search of new homes in Europe and the New World. From here band after band of refugees fanned out in different directions for places of settlement. Augsburg was something of a religious shrine to the Lutherans, for the Reformer, Martin Luther, was there first tried for heresy in 1518, after having challenged basic doctrines of the Catholic Church in the Ninety-five Theses which he tacked to the door of the Castle Church at Wittenberg on All Saints Day in 1517. When Luther was at Augsburg for the trial by Cajatan, Pope Leo X's personal emissary, he was housed in the Carmelite monastery adjoining St. Anne's Church. Twelve years later, Melanchthon confronted the German Imperial Diet, which was convened at Augsburg, with the basic doctrines of the Lutheran

Church as contained in the Augsburg Confession. In 1537, Augsburg was made a Lutheran city, only to be divided among Lutheran and Catholic after the Protestant defeat in the War of Schmalkald in 1546. At that time, six of the Lutheran churches were restored to the Catholic church, but soon thereafter Lutheran houses of worship bearing identical names were erected to adjoin the ceded edifices. In this same city, Emperor Charles V promulgated the Religious Peace of Augsburg in 1555, which left to the discretion of each prince of the Empire the decision as to whether his state was to be Lutheran or Catholic, or was to enjoy toleration of both religions.

The return of six churches to the Catholics of Augsburg was but a part of the fruit of victory in the Schmalkald war between Lutherans and Catholics in Germany. Soon thereafter the city of Augsburg was placed under a dual administrative system consisting of a Lutheran and a Catholic mayor and city council. In spite of this anomalous set-up and the practice of a joint meeting for the conduct of municipal affairs, the sessions, on the whole, were quite harmonious. About 200 years later, when the Salzburg exodus was under way and group after group of refugees converged on Augsburg, the Catholic council members could hardly be expected to co-operate in looking after the Lutherans who asked for lodging in the city. The Catholic burghers and councilmen, who naturally gave credence to the adverse reports of Firmian, claimed that these purported Lutherans who did not adhere to the Augsburg Confession might incite riots and might permanently settle in the city. To counteract such a menace, the Catholic members, who had a majority of one in the joint council, passed a resolution prohibiting more than 300 single persons from permanently settling in Augsburg. Anyone who employed even one more than the established quota was punishable by fine or imprisonment. Other oncoming refugees were to be banned from entering the city, except as they might be brought in under military guard when attending religious services.

From December 31, 1731, to August 13, 1732, a total of 6,116 refugees from Salzburg in eleven organized groups, each numbering from 100 to 940 persons, cleared by way of Augsburg. The first detachment put in an unannounced appearance in the evening of December 31, 1731. Hardly had the news of their arrival at the city gate beeen announced, when 1000 Lutherans in the city went out to meet them. Over night they were lodged in homes and inns outside the city wall. The following morning religious services were conducted for them at *Schaurichergarten,* a place for entertainment and refreshment, and at the hospital where many had been confined. After the conclusion of the garden service, most of them, chiefly men- and maid-servants, were cared for in the almshouse.

A second detachment arrived in Augsburg late on the evening of January 25, 1732. But despite the wretched health of many of the refugees, due to days of exposure to severe winter weather of snow, ice, and slush, the city council, by a majority of one, refused to have the city gate opened to them. Those who could not be accommodated in suburban homes were put up for the night in the *Schieszgraben,* an enclosed rifle range and amusement park where marksmen practiced in preparation for the annual national championship contest. The following morning religious services were held in the *Schieszgraben,* the *Friedhof* or cemetery, and the Protestant wing of the hospital.

Samuel Urlsperger, Senior Deacon and Pastor of St. Anne's, obtained permission to have the refugees, who were quartered at the *Schieszgraben* and at inns outside the city, brought into Augsburg for religious services. At five o'clock the next morning, after all had been assembled at the *Schieszgraben,* deputies and soldiers from the city appeared for organizing the march into town. The procession was led by a deputy of the city and his lieutenant, followed by a corporal and two soldiers, and then the Salzburgers followed in groups led by the inn-keepers with whom they had been housed for the night. These groups were separated from each other by spaces of 30 to 40 paces, with a soldier between to keep the groups separated, and the ones who had been quartered in the *Schieszgraben* were last in the procession.

As with a single voice, they sang their familiar songs when they marched along the road lined by cheering spectators on either side to the Goeking city gate. The street from the gate to St. Anne's had been cleared and soldiers stood guard from the gate into the church court and up to the entrance to the sanctuary. Upon entering St. Anne's the Salzburgers were welcomed by the clergy, and were seated together in the order in which they had been formed for marching into the city. In the line of march a woman was seen carrying her infant in its cradle strapped to her shoulders.

At the conclusion of the service, with cantors strategically placed, the Salzburgers were invited to sing alone without organ accompaniment, and then they were marched back to the *Schieszgraben* in the order of their arrival at St. Anne's. On the way out of St. Anne's each person, young as well as old, received a money gift, articles of clothing, Bibles, New Testaments, and a variety of Christian tracts. Outside the gate and along the road to the *Schieszgraben,* crowds again awaited them. From the beginning to the end of the performance, no untoward act occurred, and their conduct won for the Salzburgers the respect of all who witnessed the affair.

A total of 77 commemorative coins of the Salzburg exodus were cast in Germany. A description of a few of them should suffice to furnish an idea of the reverence in which the exiles were held. Some of these coins bore varying and significant inscriptions, such as: "Depart from your fatherland"; "To Prussia God has sent you"; "Go into a land which I shall show you"; "Kings shall be your servants"; and "Schools has the King of Prussia built for us." On one coin was engraved the image of Scheitberger, with the inscription, "I will myself bed my sheep," and on the reverse side was an engraving of Christ as the Good Shepherd in the midst of his flock, set in a Salzburg landscape. On another coin, Jesus was shown leading a flock of sheep, with the inscription: "My sheep shall hear my voice." In another instance an emigrant family was shown, with mountains in the background, a man and a woman, an infant in arms, and a small boy held by the hand. On the reverse side of this coin appeared a horse-drawn baggage-cart with the driver on the mount. At the top of the engraving was the Divine eye looking down upon him, and below was the inscription, "Depart and travel in peace." Still another coin portrayed the enthroned King of Prussia receiving Salzburgers, while on either side of the monarch stood an armed retainer.

CHAPTER XV

THE SALZBURGER EXODUS TO GEORGIA

THE NAME of Samuel Urlsperger is written indelibly into the annals of the settlement of the Salzburgers in Georgia, for it was through him that they were recruited for their journey to that last of the British mainland colonies. Urlsperger, as a disciple of the Halle pietist, August Hermann Francke, was concerned above all for the spiritual welfare of the Salzburgers, and no sooner had a band of them been assembled at Augsburg for departure than he and the Lutheran community of the city made every effort to prepare them mentally and spiritually for what lay ahead. From the time they left Augsburg, en route to America by way of Rotterdam and England, and even after they were settled in Georgia, Urlsperger made sure of pastoral guidance for them.

He was the descendant of a family of Urlspergers which was obliged to leave Austria on account of religion. His grandfather was a Lutheran minister, and his father was an officer in the imperial army during the Thirty Years' War. At the end of that struggle the family settled in Kirchen in the kingdom of Wuerttemberg. Samuel was educated for the ministry. In 1703 he matriculated at the University of Tuebingen, and five years later we find him at Halle where he was associated with Francke, professor of Oriental languages and a champion of Lutheran pietism. At this wellspring of pietism Francke and his disciples stressed the importance of a Christian life rather than dogmatic theological speculation. Another Halle-inspired Lutheran leader was Heinrich Melchior Muehlenberg, who settled in Pennsylvania in 1742. His title, the Patriarch of the Colonial Lutheran Church of America, was well deserved, for his journeys in Pennsylvania, New York, New Jersey, Maryland, Virginia, Carolina, and Georgia developed in the Lutherans of America a strong sense of unity.

Halle University had been founded by the pietist, Philip Jacob Spener, professor of theology at the University of Leipzig. He and a number of his theological students seceded from Leipzig and founded the University of Halle in protest against the formal theological instruction by the divinity faculty of Leipzig. Francke, a junior associate of Spener, founded the famous orphanage of Halle, often called "a ragged school." It originated in his home where he instructed a small group of orphans in the fundamentals of Christianity. When Urlsperger came to Halle the orphanage and its adjoining buildings had expanded into a community center which was dedicated to Christian living and education. Here Bible societies were founded and young men like Urlsperger, Muehlenberg, and the spiritual leaders of the Georgia Salzburgers were trained for the ministry and for foreign missionary endeavor.

From Halle Urlsperger traveled to London to serve as pastor at the Savoyan Lutheran Chapel of Prince George, heir to the English throne. Urlsperger's pastorate there led to a close association with the Anglican clergy and prominent members of the Whig Party and to membership in the "Society for the Promotion of Christian Knowledge." Two years later Urlsperger returned to his native Wuerttemberg to accept an appointment to the pastorate of the royal chapel at the city of Stuttgart. After five years of service there he was removed because he objected to the dual church affiliation, Lutheran and Calvinist, and to the immoral conduct of Duke Eberhard V of Wuerttemberg.

A prominent English merchant and a member of the Lutheran city council of Augsburg had him appointed pastor and soon thereafter in 1724, as "Senior" Pastor of St. Anne's Church. In 1730 Urlsperger was chosen a member of the Trustees for establishing the Colony of Georgia in America. Two years later, when the Salzburg exodus had reached flood tide, he was asked by the Trustees to recruit three hundred of the Salzburgers for the colony of Georgia. He agreed, on the condition that he be authorized to appoint a pastor, an assistant, and their successors to accompany them and settle with them in Georgia.

Once the Anglican clergy were assured of the exemplary character of the Salzburgers, the Society for the Promotion of Christian Knowledge solicited funds for their benefit. The Trustees agreed to bear all the expenses which might be incurred for their transportation to Georgia and for their support until they had become self-sufficient. After taking an oath of allegiance to the British crown they were guaranteed all the rights and privileges of Englishmen. All children born to them in Georgia were to be British citizens. All weapons for defense, tools, seed for planting, and live stock were to be furnished by the Trustees.

Many perplexing questions, however, needed to be answered for the Salzburgers before they would be willing to launch out upon the Georgia venture. Weighing heavily against such a venture were undoubtedly such influences as the enthusiastic reception accorded them on their recent march, the ability of many individuals to find gainful employment in cities where they were entertained, and the opportunity to settle in a familiar European environment free of religious restrictions. Once the Salzburgers had reached Protestant Germany, religion ceased to be a matter of serious concern. Even the powerful prince-bishops of Mainz, Cologne and Trier would not have dared do what was done by Firmian of Salzburg.

What perplexed these Salzburgers can best be gleaned from the answers to their queries. In Georgia they would, of course, be permitted to worship according to the dictates of their own consciences. Everything would be done in the colony to put them at ease. Neither their characteristic dress nor their language should be the cause of embarrassment to them. Their pastors, who would accompany them, could act as interpreters and their children would soon learn the English language. Free and unrestricted association with their neighbors would soon dispel any prejudice which might exist. There was no doubt but that they would be able to earn a living in the colony in the sweat of their brow. And for the overseas voyage everything would be done for their comfort and for safeguarding their health. No more than one hundred and fifty emigrants at a time would be taken aboard a transport.

They were cautioned against lending credence to discouraging rumors about the unfortunate plight of many others who had emigrated to foreign lands. The German Palatines who had gone to Carolina two decades ago had done so to escape political and personal restrictions and therefore had arrived in the colony as beggars or as indentured servants. And those Germans bound for Pennsylvania had gone in anticipation of a life of ease, which, of course, no Salzburger had any reason to expect in Georgia. Urlsperger assured his group that although some criminals had been sent to New England, New York, Barbados, Jamaica, and other colonies, none had been sent to Georgia.

Only forty-two of the two hundred and forty-seven Salzburgers, mostly from districts of Gastein and Pinzgau who had arrived at

Augsburg from Memmingen, responded favorably to the offer of the Trustees for the Colony of Georgia. From August to October 31, 1733, they were housed in homes outside the city walls. Only under military guard were they admitted to the city for regular religious services and special functions. All expenses for their sojourn at Augsburg were defrayed by funds derived from the Salzburg emigrant treasury at Ratisbon and by generous financial grants by the London Society for the promotion of Christian Knowledge. Then too the Lutheran community of Augsburg itself spared neither expense nor effort in looking after the personal comfort and spiritual well-being of the emigrants. Those who were able to read were given Bibles, hymnals, catechisms, and religious tracts. And the daily religious services of these emigrants for Georgia were attended by large numbers of Augsburgers from every walk of life. In the seven months of their residence at Augsburg, the Salzburgers, old and young alike, were led to a deeper appreciation of the faith within them, and they acquired a spiritual preparation for the voyage to America and the trying days which lay ahead.

On the morning of their departure for Rotterdam the Salzburgers were assembled at the Schieszgraben outside the city wall. Here they were received by the Lutheran mayor, a deputy of the Protestant city council, Samuel Urlsperger, and George Philip von Reck, who was the commissioner appointed to manage the affairs of the Salzburgers en route to America and to look after their settlement in Georgia. Following the farewell sermon by Urlsperger and a song service, the honored guests were showered with liberal donations. From the Augsburg Protestant organization they received five hundred Rhenish Florins,[1] one hundred and seventy-three Florins from a special collection raised by the Augsburg Lutherans, and one hundred and forty-two florins from the Salzburg refugee treasury of Ratisbon. A nobleman who wished to remain anonymous presented each emigrant with one Florin.[2] In addition, they were generously remembered with gifts of linens, household utensils, and personal necessities. Children and baggage were loaded in

---

[1]Beheim-Schwarzbach, *Friedrich Wilhelm I's Kolonisationswerk in Litauen, vornehmlich die Salzburger Kolonie* (Koenigsberg, 1879), cited in Hans Widmann, *Geschichte Salzburgs*, III, 417-419, Value of money in 1879: 8 florins equaled one gulden in 1879: one gulden = $10 in 1930.

[2]Total received was approximately $2,000.

wagons furnished gratis by the Augsburgers. Von Reck and an interim pastor, Mr. Schuhmacher, led the procession, riding in a chaise. A considerable group of Augsburg admirers followed them to Wertheim, a nearby town on the Main River. The next morning the Salzburgers embarked for the voyage down the Main to the Rhine. They were en route for twenty-seven days to Rotterdam, Holland, but, no matter how tedious was each day's journey, their spirits were kept high by a feeling of certainty that by nightfall an exhilarating reception, a restful night, and a cheerful morning adieu awaited them.

At Wertheim the emigrants were surprised to learn that a Catholic attended both their evening and morning devotional. He seemed deeply impressed by their devoutness, and upon leaving he expressed his gratitude for the privilege of attending the services. At Frankfurt, when it was learned that the Salzburgers were approaching the city, a military detachment was sent to welcome them and to lead them into the city. Here, at no expense to themselves, they were allowed to remain until they were able to recuperate from the strenuous day-by-day travel.

At Rotterdam they were joined by John Martin Boltzius and Israel Christian Gronau, who had been chosen by Urlsperger to minister to the spiritual needs of the emigrants. Both men were products of the Halle orphanage: the former had been Vicar of the Latin school of the Halle orphanage and the latter the Prefect of the same religious center.

The departure of the Salzburgers for Dover, England, was delayed by adverse winds and the stranding of their vessel on a sand bar outside the port of Rotterdam. Upon their arrival at Dover on December 21, they were greeted by the Reverend Mr. Ziegenhagen, the preacher at the royal German chapel in London, by a Trustee for the Colony of Georgia, and by an interpreter. Meanwhile, the transport was stocked with a three-months' supply of meat, vegetables, and brandy for the over-seas voyage. In port and while ashore the Society for the Promotion of Christian Knowledge assumed the financial responsibility for the entertainment of the Salzburgers. A representative of the Society gave to each person who was over twenty years of age 1 £ sterling, to each person between fifteen and twenty a lesser amount, and to all others five shillings each. Commissioner von Reck and Pastor Boltzius each was presented with £ 5 sterling and Mr. Gronau with £ 3 sterling. An anonymous donor gave to each Salzburger a half-crown.

The First Transport

A London newspaper correspondent who traveled from Rotterdam to Dover with the Salzburgers said of them:

"My fellow travellers and I were greatly impressed by them. At Dover they were entertained to dinner by the Trustees. They were seated at one table and the other guests bound for Georgia at the other. The procession of the Salzburgers into the hall was led by von Reck. Boltzius and Gronau were at the end of the procession. The Salzburgers sang as they filed into the hall and at intervals while dining. Their sincerity and their profound knowledge of the basic tenets of Christianity evinced by their answers in the catechetical hour amazed all of us. They were deeply appreciative for the slightest favor. I was convinced that any country in which they might choose to settle would, indeed, be fortunate and that Great Britain had every reason to be proud of her Georgia Salzburgers.

"Other guests bound for Georgia who were seated at the second table were deeply moved when they heard the Christian refugees invoke God's blessing before dining and thank Him for all benefits which he had bestowed upon them. At the conclusion of dinner the climax of the occasion was reached when they burst forth in singing 'Come Holy Spirit, Heavenly Dove'."[3]

From Dover the transport bearing the first Salzburgers bound for Georgia sailed on January 8, 1734, and reached the open sea three days later, but did not sight land off the coast of South Carolina until March 5. Before arrival in America several instances of excitement occurred. Early on the afternoon of January 28 all on board the vessel were panic-stricken by what seemed to be an explosion. A shipmate who was preparing meat for dinner accidentally spilled the grease from the meat into an open flame. At the very time the sailing vessel was wrapped in a cloud of smoke from the

---

[3]Cited in Samuel Urlsperger, *Ausfuehrliche Nachricht von den Salzburgischen Emigranten die sich in Amerika niedergelassen haben,* I, 50.

135

burning grease, two members of the crew were working in the powder magazine. Piercing screams of terror came from old and young alike, who feared that an explosion had occurred in the powder magazine. But Captain Coram ordered all passengers to report to the fore of the vessel and calm soon prevailed. A few days later occurred another event that was the occasion of some excitement. Around eight o'clock in the evening, what was thought to be a pirate ship was sighted. When the supposed pirate ship's captain failed to respond to Captain Coram's request that the vessel's identity be given, Captain Coram ordered a shot to be fired over the bow of the approaching vessel and all sails on the Salzburger transport to be hoisted. But the unidentified craft soon changed its course and disappeared from sight.

At Charleston, South Carolina, the Salzburgers were welcomed to America by General Oglethorpe. He had delayed his voyage back to England in anticipation of their arrival. They, as his favorite guests, arrived at Savannah Harbor on Sunday March 10, 1734. No sooner had their transport dropped anchor, than the shore batteries boomed a salute of welcome and the Savannans who had gathered on shore joined in a greeting of loud cheers. Soon thereafter, von Reck, Boltzius and several others were taken on a tour of the town and were shown its wooded areas and the newly planted garden plots. On shore the refugees were treated to fresh meat, vegetables, and good English beer. Except for von Reck, Boltzius, and Gronau, who resided at the home of the Reverend Mr. Quincy, then on a visit with his parents in London, the rest of the Salzburgers returned to the vessel for the night until temporary headquarters had been erected on shore.

They resided at Savannah from March 13, until April 7, when they moved to a place they called Ebenezer, where they made their permanent home. On the following morning they were agreeably surprised when a Jew, who held a substantial grant of land, brought them a tasty morsel of rice for their breakfast. During their sojourn in Savannah the local church was made available to the Salzburgers for their daily religious services. Their meetings never lacked interested spectators, and they were greatly pleased to have members of the twelve Jewish families of Savannah attend their services regularly. In their report to Urlsperger they expressed the hope of converting these Jews to Christianity.

136

On the day on which the Salzburgers had settled in their temporary headquarters, General Oglethorpe put in an appearance at Savannah. One of his first acts was to have von Reck set out to find a place for them to establish a permanent settlement. Von Reck soon returned and reported that he was unable to make any headway because of dense forests and treacherous swamps. On the next day, General Oglethorpe and von Reck, accompanied by Indian guides, set out in search of a suitable location. Von Reck reported in his diary that he had selected a hilly area with green pastures traversed by streams and clear cool brooks. It was twenty-one German miles from Savannah and thirty miles from the sea.

On March 20, Commissioner Zweifler and eight strong, unwed Salzburgers set out to erect a shelter to be occupied by the emigrants until they had constructed permanent cabins. They called the place Ebenezer (stone of help), meaning "Hitherto hath the Lord helped us."

Boltzius tells in his *Journal*:

"This morning early, Mr. Zweifler and eight Salzburgers, who were to go today to build the Houses, received the Sacrament, in the Presence of some others of our People. After a Psalm was sung, and Prayers said, a Sermon was preached before them out of Matt. XXII. 1. Of the Great Mercy of God toward Men, 2. Of the Way how to become meet for his Mercy. After this, the Communion was performed. The English Minister was present at the Communion; and yesterday likewise, when Mr. Rothe's Child was baptized, who was born here since our Arrival. He was very much pleased with our Communicants, and the whole Order of our Divine Service; and afterwards, at the House one of the Majistrates, who had invited him and one of us to Breakfast, he spoke in a very Christian Manner of our Communion. The rest of the Salzburgers are to receive the Sacrament next Sunday.

"Mr. Oglethorpe hath desired that one of us should go with the eight Salzburgers to our Settlement, in order to preach the Word of God to them, before they go to work and after, and because I am much taken up with writing Letters and am to administer the Sacrament to the Salzburgers who remain here, Mr. Gronau hath taken this Journey upon him."[4]

---

[4]*Op. cit.*, p. 25.

Von Reck remarked in his *Journal* of April 3:

"We came to the Village of Abercorn, at four in the afternoon; from hence, we were forced to carry our Provisions and Baggage to Ebenezer by land. April 4. I stayed at Ebenezer, and could not but commend the Diligence and Industry of the nine Salzburgers, who come before, and whose Labour God had given a Blessing unto. They had erected two good Tents, made of the Barks of Trees, one of which was forty foot long; and had cut down an abundance of Trees, in order to breathe a free Air; and besides all that they were obliged in the greatest Heats almost every Day, to walk to Abercorn, which is twelve Miles; and to carry their Utensils and daily Provisions, upon their Backs. After this God was pleased to show us a more convenient Road than the other, by which we avoided one of the greatest Brooks. April 7. The rest of the Salzburgers arrived."[5]

The Second Transport

Approximately six months after the first Salzburgers had arrived at Savannah, the Trustees announced that they were prepared to accept from forty to fifty Salzburgers or Germans for Georgia. By this time the exodus from Salzburg had declined to a mere trickle, so that the appeal was published in German cities where Salzburgers had settled. Relatives of those already in America were especially urged to take advantage of the opportunity. In September eighteen more than the desired quota had arrived at Augsburg from Memmingen, Lindau, Leutkirch, and Lipsheim, many of them skilled craftsmen. The names of all persons who had received permission from their employers and their governments to leave were recorded in the Urlsperger Journal. They were Simon Steiner, a bleacher, age thirty-six; Goerge Kogler, carpenter and excellent workman, age twenty-six; Gabriel Maurer, mason and a man of exceptional integrity, age twenty-six; Stephen Rotenberger, a mason of exceptional skill, age twenty-three and a half; Nicholas Riedelsperger, herdsman for the Augsburg infirmary, age forty-five, who was a competent cattleman; Adam Riedelsperger, a hired hand, age thirty-three; Hans Mastreuter, day laborer, age thirty-

---

[5]*Op. cit.*, p. 41.

eight; Maria Riedelsperger, servant in the Urlsperger household, thirty-two years of age. In conclusion the record stressed that all members of the party were reputable persons.

Through negotiations in Vienna, between the British representative and the Primate of the Catholic Church of Germany, the Salzburgers were accorded free and unrestricted access to Augsburg. In the few days of their abode in that city, Urlsperger and his associates did what they could in the allotted time to put the emigrants in the proper spiritual frame of mind for the venture beyond the sea. The Rev. Matthaeus Degmeyer and commissioner John von Vatt, who were chosen to direct their journey to America, joined them in Augsburg. Upon their arrival at Gravesend in England on October 27, von Vatt received a letter asking that the Salzburgers be brought to London for a public appearance at the city hall. He was told that thousands would be afforded the pleasure of seeing Christians who preferred death to a betrayal of their consciences.

In London they worshiped regularly at the German Swedish Church in Trinity Lane. Over night they were lodged on their transport and by day they resided at a place the Trustees had leased. On Sunday morning, the seventh day of November, the Lord Mayor of London sent an escort of six to lead the Salzburg group from their ship to the place of worship. The escort, von Vatt, the pastor of the Swedish church, an official representative of London, and the city marshal led the procession. Without a previous announcement a collection to the amount of forty-seven £ sterling was taken up for them at the service. From auxiliary London funds each adult received twenty £ sterling.

When the service was concluded the Salzburgers were escorted to a spacious dining hall. City constables led the way and cleared a passage for them through the crowd of spectators. In the vanguard were the trustees, von Vatt, and Pastor Degmeyer. As they marched into the hall between rows of spectators, they sang the "Battle Song of the Reformation" and other hymns. At dinner the honored guests were served by the Trustees. One of the Salzburgers remarked that he was ashamed to have such distinguished persons of wealth serve him. Another exclaimed, "Oh! Would that the Catholics of Salzburg might witness this sight, how humiliating it would be for them to see us fare so well." Following the usual musical interludes, the catechetical hour, the prayer of thanks, and the song fest, the Salzburgers marched out by organ accompaniment, singing the anthem:

"I am a worthless exile here—
Thus must my name be given—
From native land and all's that dear
For God's Word I am driven."

At the Tower of London they went aboard six craft which conveyed them to their America-bound transport. On the following day they stopped at Gravesend to stock the ship with the supplies necessary for the journey. Reverend Mr. Ziegenhagen, who had not been able to meet with the Salzburgers while they were in London, came aboard to bid them adieu and *bon voyage*. Before sailing, each of the fifty-seven emigrants over twenty years of age was awarded two £ sterling and the others slightly less.

On November 12, 1734, the ship, *Prince Edward,* having on board the Salzburgers, and the Indian chief Tomo Chichi and his entourage returning from London to Georgia, sailed for America. After a fairly calm voyage, the Prince Edward anchored in Savannah Harbor on December 27. The emigrants, on their arrival at Ebenezer on January 13, 1735, were temporarily housed in the homes of the resident Salzburgers until such time as they were able to construct homes for themselves.

The Third Transport

Von Reck, who had returned to Germany after planting the first Salzburgers at Ebenezer, was delegated by the trustees to manage the affairs of the third contingent. On August 16, 1734, when at Ratisbon, he was asked to leave for Augsburg to take over the task of organizing a third band of Salzburgers. The trustees hoped that they could be brought to London in time to embark for Georgia with General Oglethorpe. When they left Augsburg on September 7, a company of Augsburgers marched along with them to Langenweit, approximately a two-hour journey.

About a month later they arrived in London, where a total of one hundred and fifty English, German, French, and Irish were waiting to travel to Georgia with the Salzburgers. Three days after General Oglethorpe had set sail, they and the others bound for Georgia departed on the *London Merchant*.[6] After docking at Gravesend to take on supplies and clearing the English Channel on December 23, the ship was detained for the repair of a dangerous leak in its hull. When it reached the Bay of Biscay, off the coast of Spain and France, it was delayed sixty hours for another major repair. To keep it seaworthy for the remainder of the voyage, six men were needed at all times to operate the ship's pumps.

For a fortnight after January 28, the vessel was beset by vicious storms. All masts and sails had to be lowered, the rudder secured, and the helpless ship left to the merciless elements. It seemed as though each of the waves which swept relentlessly over the deck of the *London Merchant* was bent upon swallowing it and its terror-stricken passengers. Despite the wind and weather the *London Merchant* and the vessel which had sailed three days earlier arrived safely at Savannah on February 16, 1736, with a total of three hundred passengers.

Soon after the arrival of the Salzburgers, Oglethorpe was prevailed upon to lay out a new town for them in a less marshy and more accessible location. This was the "New Ebenezer," planted on a ridge called "Red Bluff" overlooking the Savannah River.

The Fourth Transport

The organization and the management of the fourth group of Salzburg emigrants assembled at Augsburg was entrusted to Johann Gottfried Mueller. It set out for Rotterdam and London on January 12, 1741. The members of this band had been recruited from Memmingen, Lindau, Bieberach, Stuttgart, and Ulm. Seven days after leaving Rotterdam the ship passed Gravesend on its way to London. At London the Salzburgers were detained for two weeks waiting for a transport.

They were entertained in London much after the manner of two previous emigrant groups. Their characteristic dress seemed to intrigue the Londoners. Visitors were usually present when the Salzburgers prepared their meals, at times even sampling dishes which were new to them. The refugees for Georgia never lacked an audience when they were dining. The trustees saw to it that they always had a liberal supply of bread, meat, beer, shortening, and other necessities.

---

[6]*Op. cit.* Urlsperger Zweyte continuation p. 823.

141

Upon leaving London, Mr. Vigera assumed the organizing duties of von Mueller. On September 18 the fourth troop of Salzburgers was on its way. They passed Dover twenty days later, and lost sight of land on October 26.

Off an island near the southwest coast of England, which was a rendezvous for Spanish pirates, a vessel was seen drifting toward the English ship. When the British captain was unable to identify it, he ordered a red flag to be hoisted on his vessel. The other in turn hoisted a Dutch flag. As the strange craft came within the range of the English captain's spy glass, he noticed a considerable number of men on board but could see no cannon. Remembering the description of pirate vessels which he had received in London, the captain ordered all men on board to arm. The transport's fifty soldiers were stationed at the foredeck, forty-four Scotsmen at mid-deck, and the Salzburg men at aftdeck. Women and children erupted in shrieks of terror when they were ordered to their cabins.

As the strange vessel drifted within voice range, the captain of the English ship with the Union Jack unfurled, demanded that the Dutch ship identify itself as to origin and destination. Failing to understand the reply, he demanded that the Dutch vessel lower a boat and send men aboard. After supplying the necessary information, they were permitted to return to their vessel without further ado.

On December 2 the vessel bearing the Salzburg emigrants anchored in the Savannah River and on the following day they were welcomed by the town magistrate. One week later, Boltzius arrived to escort them up the Savannah River to New Ebenezer. In the main the affairs of the settlement were administered by its pastor with little interference from the colonial government at Savannah.

CHAPTER XVI

EPILOGUE

THE HISTORY of Salzburg from the fall of 1731, when the *Emigrationspatent* was promulgated, until the death of Archbishop Firmian in 1774, was that of a steady decline in the spiritual and material fiber of the country. Nothing seemed to matter, as far as Firmian was concerned, so long as he could enhance his position within the hierarchy of the Catholic church, and add luster to his administration through an elaborate building-program. However, he failed to obtain the coveted office of cardinal and had to be satisfied with the pope's order that he be formally addressed in the manner of a cardinal with the title *Excelsus Principis*. In 1732 he gave little thought to the huge expense involved in the construction of the *Kapitalschwemme* (a fountain and pool) in front of the headquarters of the Cathedral chapter and in the furnishing and decorating of his *Lustschloss* (recreation castle) named *Klesheim*. Four years later, with the approval of the cathedral chapter, he built the castle of *Leopoldshorn,* named for himself, Leopold Anton Freiherr von Firmian, at a cost of 400,000 Gulden. The castle and the land which surrounded it were held in trust by the cathedral chapter as a residential estate for Firmian's impoverished relatives.

Throughout his administration he did whatever he could to blot out the remaining embers of Lutheranism in Salzburg and to guard against "heretical" infiltration from without. Persons who had been expelled but who were later permitted to return to liquidate what they could of their remaining property were placed under rigid scrutiny. Upon entering the principality they had to register with the government and submit to a careful search for censored literature. From the time they entered they were under constant surveillance to see that they attended to their business affairs without delay. No sooner had they accomplished their mission, some times even before, than they were accompanied to the frontier with orders not to return, upon penalty of being sold to Venice as galley slaves.

A like judgment awaited any exile who was caught entering Salzburg without permission. The search and seizure of censored literature continued unabated. Anyone found in possession of forbidden books or pamphlets was subject to a fine in the amount of one-tenth of the value of his property. All fines collected for such offenses were supposed to be used for the establishment and maintenance of missions in Salzburg.

In the district of Gastein alone, between 1734 and 1750, fines to the amount of 11,000 Florins[1] were collected from persons who possessed Protestant Literature. Johann Viehofer, aged 70, who owned property valued at 1420 Florins was fined 400 Florins for such an offense, and his two sons were forced from the parental home. Viehofer was made to pay the informer 50 Florins and to employ two household servants who were appointed by the government to watch and report his every act. Their discharge was subject to governmental approval. Another such offender was Georg Fritzenwalder, who was fined 300 Florins.

The systematic persecution of Protestants ended in Salzburg during the Seven Years' War (1756-1763) and all religious restrictions ceased ten years later. Almost without exception, the Protestants who reside in Salzburg today are descendants of persons who settled in the archbishopric since the last quarter of the eighteenth century. The Lutherans of the city of Salzburg completed their formal organization early in the second half of the nineteenth century.

To reduce the tension in Salzburg caused by the presence of Jesuits, Pope Clement XII requested Firmian to appoint Capuchin monks of the order of St. Francis to replace them. This task was made less difficult because of the disrepute into which Jesuits had fallen, even in Catholic countries. Everywhere they had infiltrated into the chancelleries of Europe, had intrenched themselves in educational and administrative institutions of Protestant as well as Catholic countries, and resentment against their Machiavellian tactics had been building up throughout Europe. Catholic princes, abbots, university professors, as well as monastic orders, resented and feared them.

The Capuchins who took over in Salzburg were known to be less aggressive and more tolerant than the Jesuits. Prerequisites for

---

[1]Eight Florins were worth one Gulden.

appointment were that the Capuchins be well versed in the Scriptures, in theology, and above all in debate. Their life was to be blameless and they were prohibited from accepting gifts for either charitable or personal purposes. Neither were they to wander from house to house in search of alms, nor were they to absent themselves from their mission territory without permission.

Under Firmian's rule, hypocrisy, sanctimony, and superstition pervaded the life of Salzburg. The most common objects to be seen in the archbishopric were amulets blessed by priests, which were supposed to protect against evil fortune in matters ranging from the cradle to the grave. There was hardly a household to be found which did not display blessed objects which were believed to bestow some special benefit to hearth, home, land, and goods. Education was in a state of decline, and the clergy who were supposed to lead the people were apprehensive lest literacy might breed religious dissent. A mania for honors, titles, and class distinctions was uppermost in the public mind, and at the opening of the nineteenth century bad money, poor credit, restrictions on business enterprises, and the ravages of war, which engulfed nearly all of Europe, brought Salzburg to the brink of disaster.

The bid for immigrants to fill the void left in Salzburg by the exodus failed to stem the tide toward decline. Only the less prosperous and enterprising Catholics were ready to take advantage of the alluring promises made by Firmian. Many who failed to find what they had been led to expect returned to their former homeland. Others who could not afford to leave or had nothing better to return to, and were unable to adjust themselves to the mountain environment of Salzburg, drifted into abject poverty and soon lost their identity in a strange environment. Any number of large estates with a single proprietor and without tenants or day laborers lapsed into primeval conditions. The district of Pongau lay deserted for many years, and only a few residents were to be found in its many narrow mountain-valleys.

In spite of a declining economy and a mounting volume of unpaid taxes, Firmian did nothing to curtail his mounting household and administrative expenses. Instead, he increased the taxes and made them payable in quarterly installments, but still they could not be collected. In 1732 an occupational tax and a poll tax were levied by his government and two years later a license fee was imposed on the sale of all spirituous drinks. If to these are added the tithes collected by the church and the payments for religious services and for blessed amulets, is it any wonder that the Salzburgers breathed a sigh of relief when the prince-bishopric was secularized in the first decade of the nineteenth century?

The most charitable of Firmian's critics were obliged to admit that his administration was the most inefficient of any of the prelates in a millennium of the history of the archbishopric. Many of his predecessors had been firm autocrats, but they had, nevertheless, been more efficient than he was in administrative matters. No sooner had Firmian been chosen Archbishop of Salzburg, than he entrusted affairs of state to his favorites who had no interest in the welfare of the people of the prince-bishopric. His successors who ruled Salzburg from 1744 to 1772 might have come to grips with the declining economy of their principality had it not been for the Succession Wars which began in the last years of Firmian's administration.

Hieronymus, Count Colloredo (1772-1812), the last of the prince-bishops, was an advocate of the administrative principles which had been adopted by the enlightened despots of the eighteenth century. But, even if he had possessed the determination of the ablest of those despots to cope with Salzburg's political and economic decline, his efforts would have been foiled by the disastrous wars which rocked the very foundation of European society.

During the French revolutionary and Napoleonic Wars, 1789-1814, the Austrian and French armies marched through and occupied Salzburg, each exacting a toll in money and services from a state on the brink of ruin. After the defeat of Austria by Napoleon, Salzburg, Berchtesgaden and a part of Bavaria were awarded to Austria in 1797, by the terms of the Treaty of Campo Formio. This was to compensate Austria for the loss of the territory of Lombardy in Italy, which Napoleon had previously incorporated into the Cisalpine Republic. The terms of the treaty were not enforced, for almost immediately after negotiating the treaty Napoleon was preoccupied with preparations for his Egyptian campaign and his fruitless efforts to make himself master of the Near East. Soon after his return from Egypt and his coup d'état, November 9, 1799, which gave him the mastery of France, Napoleon again went to war against Austria and other members of the coalition that had been organized to save the political integrity of Europe. Following his defeat of Austria, he dictated the terms of the treaty at Lunéville, December 26, 1802. By this treaty he awarded an enlarged Salzburg, including Berchtesgaden and a part of Bavaria, to Ferdinand, brother of Francis I of Austria, whom Napoleon had removed from the Grand Duchy of Tuscany in Italy. On February 18 of the following year the subjects of Archbishop Hieronymus were absolved of their oath of allegiance to him and were ordered to pledge their fealty to Ferdinand; in addition, all church lands were secularized and Salzburg ceased to be a church state. After December 30, 1805, the principality with Berchtesgaden was transferred to Austria, but several years later, in 1809, Napoleon annexed it to Bavaria because Austria had joined a coalition against him. In 1816, soon after the overthrow of Napoleon, the administration by Bavaria ceased, and since then Salzburg has been a province of Austria.

No matter where the Salzburgers settled permanently, whether in Europe or America, their industry and their loyalty to government in their new homes measured up to the fondest hopes of their patrons. The status of the Georgia Salzburgers can be gleaned from a letter written on June 6, 1741, and addressed to their fellow countrymen who had been settled in Lithuania, a province of the kingdom of Prussia:

In Christ dearly beloved countrymen, brothers, sisters and blood relatives:

As of this date there are about eighty Salzburger families in Ebenezer, Georgia. Most of whom were recruited in the German cities of Augsburg, Memmingen, Lindau and others. We are all permitted to pursue the vocations of our choice. Each householder has a fifty-acre grant of land. Farming seems to be developing in a manner similar to what it was in Salzburg. God has blessed us with cattle, hogs, and poultry and we do not lack for milk, lard, meat, and grain. Our forests abound in game and fowl and our streams in a variety of fishes. We may fish and hunt to our heart's desire; but alas, the demands which this primeval environment exacts of us afford us little time for fishing and hunting. In spite of the fertility of the soil much time is consumed clearing the land of huge trees, dense underbrush, and weeds, a task which becomes less burdensome from season to season. Though the land is fairly flat and without obstructive rocks it is traversed by a network of roots which impedes the cultivation of the soil. The water of the springs and streams in Ebenezer is clear and healthful. Our settlement is strategically located for travel by water to and from the market. Last week we built the first mill in this region on one of the streams which traverse the colony. Old and young alike thank God for the achievement, We are now engaged in getting settled. God is most considerate of us, for he has instilled all Christendom with a charitable interest in our well-being not only as we traveled through Germany but also in our journey to England and to Ebenezer in Georgia. Our friends have not ceased in their beneficence toward us. But a few days ago three chests containing linen, shoes, books, and medicines arrived for us from Europe. We have every reason to praise God for his many blessings but above all for having spared us of the ravages of the war in which England and France are engaged.[2]

In response to the letter addressed to the Salzburgers in Lithuania, Adam Fritscher, a Prussian schoolmaster, replied, January 5, 1742:

> In the name of our beloved Savior, dearly beloved friends, brothers, and sisters in Christ; I must admit . . . that we have fared well spiritually and bodily, something we could not have expected in Salzburg.
>
> P.S. Dear countrymen, do answer this my humble letter and cheer us; I must confess that the glow of one ember inevitably increases the warmth of the other. Hallelujah, Amen!

In a later letter, addressed to the Georgia Salzburgers, Rupert Seidler, a schoolmaster, speaks of persons after whom the Ebenezer Salzburgers inquired in the letter of June 6, 1741. He found them settled in various places and all those mentioned were doing well either as farmers or as artisans. In it he continues:[3]

---

[2]Samuel Urlsperger, *Achte Continuation der ausfuehrlichen Nachricht Salzburgischen Emigranten die sich in Amerika niedergelassen haben*, pp. 984 ff.
[3]Samuel Urlsperger, *op. cit.*, pp. 997 ff.

The hospitalized Salzburgers are well cared for and all the others are enjoying God's blessing. They have the reputation of being outstanding colonists. They are faithful, industrious, and obedient subjects of our most gracious king and lord. As farmers and cattlemen they are contributing to the agricultural progress of Lithuania.

Frederick II of Prussia praised them for their piety, technical skill, prompt payment of financial obligations, and their ability as horse breeders. It was generally recognized that they had given an excellent account of themselves in spiritual and material matters. They rehabilitated a Lithuania which had been laid waste by war and pestilence.

The property which the Lithuanian Salzburgers had been obliged to leave behind at the time of their expulsion was valued at 4,000,000 Gulden; in addition to this a tax of 1,500,000 Gulden was collected from them at the same time. The envoy of Frederick II of Prussia, sent to Salzburg to salvage what he could of their property, succeeded in selling only a small part of their holdings.

All traces of the hundreds of Duerrnbergers from Salzburg who settled in Holland soon disappeared. Unable to adjust themselves to the "thick, heavy" air of their new home bordering the North Sea, many soon died of disease. Others fled, and the few who remained were fused with the native population. The Dutch government, which had gone to considerable expense in bringing them from Ratisbon to Holland, claimed that those who left did so because they were too lazy to work. The refugees, on the contrary, claimed that once they had been settled they were neglected by the Dutch. Some of them returned to Germany while others joined their relatives in Prussia.

A similar situation existed in Hanover, where about nine hundred Berchtesgadeners had been settled through the efforts of King George of England and of Hanover. The majority of them were skilled craftsmen unable to ply their trades. Many were discontented because it was impractical for them to settle together with their kin.

After some delay, many of the skilled craftsmen were permitted to go to Nuernberg, where they contributed to the rise of the city as a toy-manufacturing center. Others found their way to Berlin, where they were employed as woodcarvers and as cotton textile workers.

Since 1816 the growth of the city of Salzburg has been quite rapid. In spite of the events in the history of Europe in the nineteenth and the twentieth century and the great fire of 1818, its special character has survived. The devastation wrought by World War II has all but disappeared. The author cannot refrain from closing with the words of Franz Fuhrmann in his *Salzburg and Its Churches*:[4]

And now, let us look at the city before us, as it lies between the rocky heights of the two hills, the Kapuzinerberg and the Moenchsberg, which give it its most characteristic silhouette. Let us note the curve, rising and falling, as the river, descending from the mountains, flows continuously and irresistibly through the city to form its living axis. Let us feast our eyes on the green line of forest which, following the river Salzach, extends right down into the heart of the town. And in doing so, we shall realize that this characteristc silhouette owes its unique and lovely design to the haughty towers and to some churches of which the main structure rises above the level of the surrounding roofs; and that this magic symphony of architecture and nature, somewhat like an orchestra of wind instruments, swells in a crescendo of sound and reaches its finale in the wide terraces of the Fortress.

[4]Fuhrmann, *op. cit.*, p. 6.

APPENDIX

A register of the names of all persons who settled and died at Ebenezer and New Ebenezer from the first settlement in 1734 to May 19, 1739 was prepared by Pastors Boltzius and Gronau. They reported: "It is evident that quite a gap exists between the 300 colonists promised and the total number at present residing at New Ebenezer."[1]

Of First Transport

1. Johann Martin Boltzius, Gertrude his assistant, Samuel Leberecht his son 2½ years of age.
2. Israel Christian Gronau, Catharina his assistant, Anna Elizabeth his daughter, 8 months of age.
3. Peter Gruber, Maria his wife (widow of Moszhammer)
4. Thomas Geschwandel, Sibylla his wife (widow of Resch) Margaretha, daughter 7 years of age.
5. Leonard Rauner, Maria Magdalena, his wife, Matthias, son 14 years of age, Maria, daughter 7 years of age.
6. Georg Schweiger, Eva Regina his wife, Catharina, daughter 6 weeks of age.
7. Margaretha Schweghofer, widow, Maria a daughter 13 years of age, Thomas, son 11 years of age and Ursula, daughter 7 years of age.
8. Martin Hertzog.
9. Christian Leimberger.
10. Simon Reiter, Margarethe Huber, an orphan.
11. Christoph Ortmann, schoolmaster, Juliana his wife.

Total 28.

Second Transport

12. Simon Steiner, Gertrude his wife.
13. Ruprecht Kalcher, Margaretha his wife, Ursula daughter 4½ years of age, and Maria, daughter 5 months old.

---

[1]Urlsperger, *op. cit.*, Vierte Continuation, pp. 2307-2312.

14. Thomas Pichler, Margareta his wife, daughter 4 years of age.
15. Stephan Rotenberger, Catharina, his wife, Susanna, daughter 5¼ years of age.
16. Matthias Burgsteiner, Agatha, his wife, Ruprecht, son 4 years of age.
17. Ruprecht Steiner, Maria his wife, Christian, son 1½ years of age.
18. Ruprecht Eichberger, Maria his wife, Catharine, daughter 2½ years of age.
19. Matthias Brandner, Maria his wife, Maria daughter 4 years of age.
20. Veit Lemmenhofer, Maria his wife.
21. Bartholomew Reiser, Maria his wife, Michael son 18 years of age, Balthasar, son 15 years of age, Georg son 13 years of age.
22. Veit Landfelder, Ursula his wife, Agatha, daughter 7 years of age.
23. Hans Maurer, Catharina, his wife, Elizabeth, daughter 1¼ years of age.
24. Thomas Bacher, Maria his wife, Maria, daughter 12 years of age, Apollonia, daughter 10 years of age.
25. Georg Kogler, Barbara his wife, Maria, daughter 5 months of age.
26. Ruprecht Riedelsperger, Anna his wife, Johannes, son 6 months of age.
27. Christian Riedelsperger.
28. Georg Sanftleben.
29. Gabriel Bach.
30. Gabriel Maurer.
31. Bartholomew Zant.
32. Christian Heszler.
33. Jacob Schartner.
34. Georg Brueckner.
35. Ruprecht Zimmermann.
36. Paul Zittrauer.
37. Carl Sigismund.
38. Heinrich Bischof, an English boy in the service of the preacher.

Total 59.

152

39. Hans Schmidt, Catharina his wife, Barbara, daughter 8 months of age.
40. Hans Floerel, Anna Maria his wife.
41. Johann Spielbiegler, Rosina his mother.
42. Johann Cronberger, Gertrude his wife, Anna Maria daughter 8 months of age.
43. Leonhardt Krause, Barbara his wife.
44. Michael Rieser, Anna Maria widowed Steger (in) Gottlieb, son 4 years of age.
45. Joseph Ernst, Maria his wife, Susanna, daughter 7 years of age, Johann Ludwig, son 4 months of age.
46. Doroth. Helfenstein, widow, Maria Friederica, daughter 18 years of age, Johann Friedrich, son 16 years of age, Maria Christina, daughter 14 years of age, Johann Jacob, son 12 years of age, Jaramia, son 10 years of age, Johannes, son 6 years of age.
47. Friedrich Mueller, Anna Christina his wife, Johann Paul, son 18 years of age, Margareta, daughter 15 years of age, Elizabeth daughter 13 years of age, Maria Magdalena, daughter 6 years of age.
48. Dorothea Amsdorf, widow, Peter, son 16 years of age, Maria Margaretha, daughter 12 years of age, Dorothea, daughter 9 years of age.
49. Andreas Grimminger, Catharina, daughter 4½ years of age.
50. Frantz Hernberger, Justina, his wife.
51. Carl Floerel.
52. Peter Reiter.
53. Martin Lackner.
54. Matthias Zettler.
55. Joseph Leitner.
56. Gottlieb Christ.
57. Johann Pletter.
58. Barbara Mauer (in) maiden lady.
59. Susanna Haberfehner (in), 15 years of age, orphan, Catharina Holtzer, 15 years of age.

Total 52.

Following persons have joined the congregation (Gemeine) Ambrosius Zueblin & Jacob Zublin, the brothers from St. Gallen. (Herr) Mr. Thilo, (Medicus).
Johann Roloinson, an English lad a servant at the orphanage. Five families of Germans, six girls and an elderly widow have joined the community as servants.

Total 21

Grand Total 160.

Deaths in the community of Salzburg from the time of our arrival to date. May 19, 1739.

1734

1. Tobias Lackner — 40
2. Matthias Mittensteiner — 41
3. Balthasar Fleisz — 27
4. Lorentz Huber — 54
5. Maria his wife — 52
6. Maria Reiter(in) — 27
7. Matthis Braumberger — 31
8. Hans Gruber — 45

1735

9. Christian Steiner — 30
10. Sebastian Glantz — 43
11. Margaretha Geschwandel — 23
12. Anna Schweiger — 26
13. Ruprecht Schoppacher — 49
14. Johann Madereiter — 49
15. Hans Moszhammer — 36
16. Simion Reuschgott — 24
17. Barbara Kraher — 39
18. Christian Schweigert — 24

1736

19. Sabina Grimmiger — 26
20. Paul Schweighofer — 44
21. Andreas Bauer — 24
22. Frantz Haberfehner — 40
23. Thomas Offenecker — 30
24. Georg Felser — 50
25. Anna Regina Zweifler — 44
26. Joh. Jai. Helfenstein — 57
27. Maria Haberfehner — 40
28. Nicol. Riedelsperger — 48
29. Adam Riedelsperger — 38

1737

30. Andr. Lorentz Arnsdorf — 60
31. Paul Lemmonhofer — 21
32. Joh. Simon Miller — 18
33. Susanna Holtzer — 48
34. Anna Maria Riescr — 25

1738

35. Maria Pichler — 30

Children

1734

1. Magdalena Huber — 15 yrs.

1735

2. Hans Huber — 10 yrs.
3. Marg. Schoppacher — 9 wks.
4. Maria Huber — 8 yrs.
5. Thomas Geschwandel — 2 hrs.
6. Georg. Schweiger — sev. hrs.
7. Maria Schoppacher — 2 yrs.
8. Maria Eichelberger — soon after baptism
9. Cathar. Eichelberger — soon after baptism
10. Agatha Steiner — 2 wks.
11. Rupr. Rottenberger — 10 dys.
12. Wolfg. Rottenberger — 13 dys.

1736

13. Joh. Jacob Schmidt — 2 yrs.
14. Margar Steiner — sev. hrs.
15. Matthias Steiner — 1 day
16. Anna Cath. Offnecker — 10 wks.
17. Johann Reidelsperger — 7 wks.
18. Cathar. Arnsdorf — 9 wks.
19. Adam Lemmenhofer — 9 mos.
20. Cathar. Gronau — 10 wks.

Andrea Piltz, Sibylla his wife
Casper Graniwetter, Anna Catharina his wife
Martin Lackner, Catharina Barbara
Georg Eigel, Ursula his wife and five children
Balthasar Bacher, Christina his wife
Michael Haberer, Anna Barbara, an infant
Georg Kogler, Barbara his wife
Two children
Bernhard Glocker, Elizabeth his wife, three children
Walburga Crellin and step-daughter
Simon Riser, Magdalena his wife
Maria Kunlin, widow, and infant
Herr Johann Ludwig Mayer, Elizabeth his wife
Johnn George Meyer
Mattaeus Bacher, Christina his wife and a widowed daughter
Peter Kohleisen, Maria his wife
George Glaner, Gertrude his wife
Hans Maurer, Maria his wife
David Eichberger, Anna Maria his wife
Johann Scheraus, Maria Helena his wife and a child
Johann George Kocher, Apallonia his wife and a boy
Veit Lechner, Magdalina his wife and a young girl
Ruprecht Schrempf and a step-son
Johann Scheffler, Catharina his wife
Magdalena Rouer
Barbara Brickl
Barbara Steinbacher
Christina Haeuszler
Apollonia Kreder[3]

---

[2]*Ibid.*, Zehnte Continuation, pp. 1834, 1835.
[3]*Ibid.*, Zehnte Continuation, pp. 1834, 1835.

1. Gruber, 22 acres of corn; 2 acres of beans; 10 acres of potatoes.
2. Geschwandel, 19 acres of corn; 2 acres of beans; 6 acres of potatoes.
3. Herzog, 15 acres of corn; 1 acre of beans; 7 acres of potatoes.
4. Limberger, 20 acres of corn; 1½ acres of beans; 6 acres of potatoes.
5. Rauner, 19 acres of corn; 2 acres of beans; 2 acres of potatoes.
6. Simon Reiter, 19 acres of corn; 2 acres of beans; 12 acres of potatoes.
7. Rheinlaender, 20 acres of corn; 4 acres of potatoes.
8. Steph. Reidelsperger, 5 acres of corn; 5 acres of potatoes.
9. Schweiger, 7 acres of corn; 3 acres of potatoes.
10. Adam Reidelsperger, 5½ acres of corn; 6 acres of potatoes.
11. Simon Steiner, 6 acres of corn; 1½ acres of beans; 2 acres of potatoes.
12. Kolcher, 6 acres of corn; 1 acre of beans; 2 acres of potatoes.
13. Pichler, 5½ acres of corn; 1½ acres of beans; 6 acres of potatoes.
14. Rothenberger, 4 acres of corn; 1 acre of beans; 1 acre of potatoes.
15. Rupr. Steiner, 12 acres of corn; 3 acres of beans; 6 acres of potatoes.
16. Eischberger, 4 acres of corn; 1 acre of beans; 6 acres of potatoes.
17. Burgsteiner, 9 acres of corn; 1½ acres of beans; 2 acres of potatoes.
18. Brandner, 8 acres of corn; 1½ acres of beans; 5 acres of potatoes.
19. Veit Lemmenhoffer, 5 acres of corn; 1½ acres of beans; 3 acres of potatoes.
20. Balthasar Reiser, 3 acres of corn; 1 acre of beans; 1½ acres of potatoes.
21. Landfelder, 5 acres of corn.
22. Bacher, 11 acres of corn; 4 acres of beans; 4 acres of potatoes.

23. Christ Riedelsperger, 2 acres of corn; 4 acres of potatoes.
24. Sanftleben, 2½ acres of corn; 1½ acres of beans; 2 acres of potatoes.
25. Bach, 1 acre of corn; 2 acres of potatoes.
26. Paul Lemmenhoffer, 4½ acres of corn; 1½ acres of beans; 3 acres of potatoes.
27. Hans Maurer, 5 acres of corn; 1 acre of beans; 2 acres of potatoes.
28. Gabrial Maurer, 4 acres of corn; 1 acre of beans; 2 acres of potatoes.
29. Zant, 2 acres of corn; 1 acre of beans; 2 acres of potatoes.
30. Hesler, 4 acres of corn.
31. Maggizer, 3 acres of corn.
32. Bruckner, 3 acres of corn; 3 acres of potatoes.
33. Zimmermann, 3 acres of corn; 1 acre of beans; 1½ acres of potatoes.
34. Kogler, 2 acres of corn; 1½ acres of beans; 2 acres of potatoes.
35. Rupr. Zittrauer, 5 acres of corn; 1 acre of beans; 1 acre of potatoes.
36. Paul Zittrauer, 4½ acres of corn; 1 acre of beans.
37. Hans Floerel, 2½ acres of corn; 1 acre of potatoes.
38. Carl Florel, 3½ acres of corn; 5 acres of potatoes.
39. Lackner

TOTALS: 22½ acres of corn; 39 acres of beans; 130 acres of potatoes.

Report of Pastors Bolzius and Gronau, made December 31, 1736, in response to the request of General Oglethorpe.[4]

---

[4]Urlsperger, *op. cit.*, Zweyte Continuation, p. 801.

CROP REPORT (IN BUSHELS) OF PLANTERS AT EBENEZER[5]

1. Rupr. Steiner, corn, 90 bu.; beans, 12 bu.; rice, 20 bu.; potatoes, 3 bu.
2. Christ. Leinberger, corn, 100 bu.; beans, 16 bu.; rice, 20 bu.; potatoes, 3 bu.
3. Christ. Hesler, corn, 33 bu.; beans, 2 bu.; rice, 12 bu.
4. Matth. Brander, corn, 91 bu.; beans, 10 bu.; rice, 15 bu.; potatoes, 11 bu.
5. Ich. Pletter, corn, 40 bu.; beans, 4 bu.; rice, 6 bu.
6. Andr. Grimmiger, corn, 80 bu.; beans, 6 bu.; rice, 18 bu.; potatoes, 8 bu.
7. Rupr. Zittrauer, corn, 60 bu.; rice, 26 bu.
8. Paul Zittrauer, corn, 60 bu.; beans, 10 bu.; rice, 10 bu.; potatoes, 5 bu.
9. Rupr. Eischberger, corn, 50 bu.; rice, 12 bu.; potatoes, 8 bu.
10. Rupr. Zimmerebaner, corn, 95 bu.; beans, 7 bu.; rice, 25 bu.; potatoes, 5 bu.
11. Mart. Kaesemeier, corn, 32 bu.; beans, 5 bu.; rice, 10 bu.; potatoes, 11 bu.
12. Jch. Flerel, corn, 70 bu.; beans, 5 bu.; rice, 10 bu.; potatoes, 3 bu.
13. Carl Flerel, corn, 70 bu.; beans, 5 bu.; rice, 20 bu.; potatoes, 4 bu.
14. Jhon. Gschwandel, corn, 70 bu.; beans, 12 bu.; rice, 30 bu.; potatoes, 9 bu.
15. Jch. Maurer, corn, 50 bu.; beans, 8 bu.; rice, 9 bu.
16. Gabr. Maurer, corn, 90 bu.; beans, 7 bu.; rice, 15 bu.; potatoes, 2 bu.
17. Mart Lackner, corn, 70 bu.; beans, 6 bu.; rice, 30 bu.
18. Joh. Schmidt, corn, 50 bu.; beans, 4 bu.; rice, 18 bu.; potatoes, 4 bu.
19. Simon Reiter, corn, 100 bu.; beans, 10 bu.; rice, 20 bu.; potatoes, 8 bu.
20. Peter Reiter, corn, 70 bu.; beans, 10 bu.; rice, 18 bu.; potatoes, 9 bu.
21. Georg. Kogler, corn, 60 bu.; beans, 10 bu.

[5]Urlsperger, *op. cit.*, 10th Continuation, p. 1775.

22. Georg. Bruckner, corn, 50 bu.; beans, 6 bu.; rice, 7 bu.; potatoes, 3 bu.
23. Leonh. Crause, corn, 80 bu.; beans, 10 bu.; rice, 24 bu.; potatoes, 6 bu.
24. Georg. Schwaiger, corn, 100 bu.; beans, 2 bu.; rice, 24 bu.; potatoes, 2 bu.
25. Veit. Lemmenhoffer, corn, 50 bu.; beans, 6 bu.; rice, 16 bu.; potatoes, 10 bu.
26. Thomas Bacher, corn, 100 bu.; beans, 9 bu.; rice, 9 bu.; potatoes, 9 bu.
27. Heinrich Bishop, corn, 56 bu.; beans, 1 bu.; rice, 10 bu.
28. Matth. Burgsteiner, corn, 56 bu.; beans, 1 bu.; rice, 30 bu.
29. Carl Siegmund Ott, corn, 60 bu.; rice, 20 bu.
30. Thom. Pichler, corn, 50 bu.; beans, 6 bu.; rice, 8 bu.; potatoes, 2 bu.
31. Joseph Leitner, corn, 20 bu.; beans, 3 bu.; rice, 12 bu.
32. Joh. Cornberger, corn, 80 bu.; beans, 15 bu.; rice, 15 bu.; potatoes, 8 bu.
33. Barthel Reiser, corn, 120 bu.; beans, 10 bu.; rice, 15 bu.; potatoes, 1 bu.
34. Maria Gruber (in), corn, 22 bu.
35. Barthol Zant, corn, 30 bu.
36. Joh. Paul Mueller, corn, 100 bu.; beans, 5 bu.; rice, 40 bu.; potatoes, 2 bu.
37. Friedr. Ludw. Nett, corn, 20 bu.
38. Chrph. Ortmann, corn, 30 bu.; beans, 2 bu.
39. Christ. Reidelsperger, corn, 60 bu.; beans, 1 bu.; rice, 1 bu.
40. Michel Reiser, corn, 40 bu.; rice, 5 bu.
41. Veit Landfelder, corn, 44 bu.; rice, 12 bu.
42. Christ. Colmann Rheinlaender, corn, 80 bu.; beans, 3 bu.
43. Maria Magd. Rauer (in) corn, 50 bu.; beans, 3 bu.
44. Chrph. Rotenberger, corn, 30 bu.; rice, 12 bu.
45. Georg Sanftleben, corn, 80 bu.; beans, 15 bu.; rice, 15 bu.; potatoes, 4 bu.

46.　Joseph Ernst, corn, 40 bu.; beans, 9 bu.
47.　Rupr. Kalcher, corn, 170 bu.; beans, 20 bu.; rice, 2 bu.;
　　　potatoes, 2 bu.
48.　Michel Schneider, corn, 12 bu.; beans, 2 bu.
49.　Joh. Georg. Held, corn, 12 bu.

TOTALS - Corn, 3,129 bu.; beans, 287 bu.; rice, 651 bu.; potatoes, 139 bu.

Reported Wed., Nov. 18, 1741 in response to a requirement of the government at Savannah.

THREE INTERESTING SALZBURG CUSTOMS

A Wedding Celebration

Long before the three to four days of a wedding celebration a Platzmeister, master of ceremonies, set out to invite the guests for the occasion. Bedecked with bright colored ribbons the Platzmeister, on a spirited mount, rode from house to house extending an invitation for the wedding to the villagers.

At the appointed hour guests, relatives and the bridal party assembled at a specified place preparatory to the march to the village church. After a brief devotional service they all marched in procession to the village church. The Platzmeister took the lead, followed by the bridal party, relatives and invited guests. A marshal riding a ribbon-bedecked horse rode well in advance of the procession. It was his duty to maintain order on the way to the border of the village, for any untoward act on the way was believed to bode an evil omen for the future of the bride and groom. Having reached the village the marshal dismounted, held out his cap and before the party could proceed to the church each person was required to tip him.

The real celebration which followed the ceremony featured music and dancing. Most important was the bridal dance at which each young man present was privileged to dance with the bride upon the payment of a fee which was applied toward the payment of the musicians or toward the purchase of household necessities for the bride. In many of the villages all the animals which belonged to the bride were brought into the dance hall.

The favorite dance was the Comsoledanz.

At this the dancers all sang.

Comsoledanz, comsoledanz
De Mutter schlacht de ole Gans.
(The mother kills the old goose)
De Vader nemst dem Stevelschacht
(The father takes hold of the top of his boot)
On haut de Mutter det ledder torecht.
(And with the boot he prepares the mother's hide)

162

At the wake following a death the young folks gathered at the home of the deceased to sing each night until the corpse had been removed for burial. The shroud was to be free of labels and of pins of any description to enable the spirit to leave the funeral dress. Legend had it that soon after death the spirit of the departed would once more return to his home. The saying was that "the departed will return to dine." Acordingly after the funeral the family table was set with a place reserved for the deceased. At the door was placed a basin of water and a guest towel to enable the departed one to wash his hands before dining.

Not to detain the returned visitor for too long a time the members of the family made haste to eat and clear the table. Then usually two of the nearest of kin arose quietly and accompanied the guest to the border of the village. A bundle of straw was then placed on the ground in order that the invisible guest might rest before continuing on his journey. The two companions united in the Lord's Prayer before returning home where a banquet attended by the villagers awaited them.

Harvest Celebration

When the last of the grain had been cut the harvest hands marched to the manor-house with scythes in hands. The lead couple bore a crown made of sheaths of grain and intertwined with bright ribbons as the harvester marched to the door of the manor. At the portal all sharpened their scythes until the lord made an appearance. They then crowned him and sang.

Wir bringen dem Herrn eine Krone aus Korn.
(We bring the lord a crown made of corn)
Sie ist gewachsen unter Dirtel und Dorn
(It has grown amid thistle and thorn)
Hat ausgestanden Schnee, Wind und Regen
(Has resisted snow, wind and rain)
Wir wuenschen dem Herrn einen tausendfachen Segen.
(We wish the Lord a thousandfold blessing.)
Sociel Aehrchen (Ear of grain)
Sociel Paerchen (Pair)

Sociel Koerner (Grains)
Sociel Scheffel (Measure)
Und alle die davon essen
(And all who eat of it)
Moege Gott unsern Herrn, nicht verlassen.
(May they God our Lord never forsake.)

BIBLIOGRAPHY

Only the sources actually consulted are listed.

Acta. *Die wegen der Salzburgischen Emigration in Memmigen angestellte Cofrenz und die von Seiten der Reichsstadt Augsburg beschlossene Abordnung 1732.* Andreas, Willy, *Deutschland vor der Reformation. Eine Zeitwende.* (Stuttgart 1948). Arnold, C. Fr., *Die Ausrottung des Protestantismus in Salzburg unter Erzbischof Firmian u. seinen Nachfolgern,* (Halle 1900). *Ausfuehrliche Historie der Emigranten oder der Vertriebenen Lutheraner aus dem Erzbistum Salzburg,* (Leipzig 1732). (These are bulky volumes of contemporary pamphlet literature on the expulsion and the wanderings of the banished Salzburgers.) Aumueller, Friedrich, *Geschichte der Evangelischen in Salzburger Land von 15ten Jahrhundert,* (Salzburg 1913). Baum, Johann H., *Der Salzburgischen Emigranten freudenmutige u. hoechst-gesegnete Wanderschaft in die koeniglich-Preussische Lande,* (1735). Buehler, Adolph, *Salzburg seine Monumente u. seine Fuersten,* (Salzburg 1873). Campe, Christian, *Kurzer u. liebreicher Anspruch ... an die unschuldig-verjagte Salzburger.* Celezki, Johann F. and others, *Wie die am 23 August 1732 ... die Stadt Zerbst ... Salzburger aufgenommen u. bewirtet etc. Chronologische Register ueber die Acta, Die Salzburger Emigranten betreffend 1731-1745,* (5 MS Vols.). Clausz, H., *Oestreichische Salzburgische Emigranten in d. Grafschaft Oettingen,* (1732). Dictatum Ratisbonae die 20, Feb. 1731, per Chur-Sachsen, *An Seine Hoch-lobliches Corpus Evangelicorum zu Regensburg. Der om Salzburg, Symbol u. Wirklickeit,* (Salzburg 1959). Eckhard, Paul J., *Christliches Muertyr-Buch.* Emerton, E., *Medieval History,* (New York 1894). Eszich, M. Johann G., *Ermunterung u. Trost-Rede an eine zahlreiche Versammlung der nach Preussen gehenden Salzburgischen Emigranten,* (Augsburg 1732). Fischer, Johann Gottlieb, *Reisebeschreibung derer Emigranten nach Cadfand im Hollaendischen Flandern,* (Leipzig 1734). Frankenstein, Jacob A., *Unmassgebliche Gedanken ueber das emigrations-Recht wegen der Religion 1689-1733.* Fuhrmann, Franz, *Salzburg and its Churches,* (Vienna 1950). Gaspari, G. B. *Aktenmaeszige Geschichte der beruehmten*

Salzburgischen Emigranten, (Salzburg 1790). Gefroerer, Aug. F., *Geschichte des achzehnten Jahrhunderts,* (Schaffhausen). Brantley, R. L., *The Salzburgers in Georgia,* (Georgia Hist. Quarterly *XIV,* 214-225). Gebhardt, Bruno, *Handbuch d. Deutschen Geschichte,* 2 Vols. (Stuttgart 1954). Goecking, Gerhard, *Salzburgischen Emigrations Geschichte,* (Leipzig 1734). Groeschel, Karl, *Exculanten in Stadt u. Bezirk Weizenburg u. Dekonat Haidenheim,* (Weizenburg 1935), Guehling, Johann F., *Die Salzburger Emigrannten . . . in die Koeniglich-Preussiche Lande,* (Nuernberg). Hahn, Johann F. C., *Der Goettliche Befehl an die Evangeligen Kirchen,* (Pamphlet of 34 pp.). Hauk, Albert, *Kirchengeschichte Deutschlands,* (Leipzig 1906). Henke, Heinrich, *Kirchengeschichte des 18ten Jahrhunderts,* (Braunschweig 1820). Hochstetter, Friederich, *Die Austreibung der evangelischen Salzburger im Jahre 1731,* (Berlin 1931). Huhn, Johann B., *Denkmal Goettlicher Guete . . .* Addresses and sermons). Kleinknecht, Conrad D., *Zuverlaessige Nachricht . . . von den Evangelischen Colonisten zu Ebenezer in Amerika.* Koeniglich-Preuszisches Patent, (Berlin, Feb. 1732). Kraemer, Johann M., *Neueste u. Richtigste Nachricht von der Landschaft Georgia in d. Engellandischen Amerika,* (1746). *Kurze Historie der Evangelischen Emigranten wie die Goetliche Providenz dieselben . . . aus dem Erzbistum Salzburg in ein Land gefuehrt worin Milch u. Honig der evang. Wahrheit fliesset,* (Pamphlet of 88 pp.). Lamprecht, Karl, *Deutsche Geschichte,* (Freiburg 1940). Lenkitsch, Wilhelm, *Die Salzburger in Ostpreussen,* (Koenigsberg 1932). Loesche, George, (Editor) *Jahrbuch der Gesellschaft fuer d. Geschichte d. Protestantismus in ehemaligen u. im neuen Oesterreich,* 52 Jahrgang, (Leipzig 1931). Martin, Franz, (Editor) *Mitteilung der Gesellschaft fuer Salzburger Landskunde,* Vols. 67-69, (Salzburg 1930). Mauelshagen, Carl, *American Lutheranism Surrenders to Forces of Conservatism,* (Athens 1936). Mittler, U. Sohn, (Editor) *Korrespondenzblatt des Gesammtvereins d. deutschen Geschichte u. Altertumsvereine,* (Berlin 1929). *Nachricht von einiger Salzburger Emigranten,* (A series of pamphlets ranging from 12 to 48 pp.). Moser, D., *Der Aktenmaessige Bericht von der jetztmaligen schweren Vervolgungen deren Evan. im Erzbischoftum Salzburg,* (Frankfurt u. Leipzig 1732). Muthmann, Johann, *Salfeldische Freude ueber die denen Salzburger Emigranten.* Ortfelder, Johann K. F., *Die evangelischen Salzburger, ihre Auswanderung nach Preussen,* (Naumburg 1857). Panse, Karl,

Geschichte der Auswanderung der evangelischen Salzburger, (Leipzig 1827), and *Geschichte der evangelischen Salzburger in den Jahren* 1731; '32, '33, (Leipzig 1832). Peyffer, Franc X., *Die Freude der protestantischen Kirchen an denen Salzb. Emigranten Angefochten. A Satire.* (Augsburg 1733). Prinziger, A., *Die Ansiedlung der Salzburger im Staate Georgia in Nord Amerika,* (Vorgetragen in der Gesellschaft fuer Salzburger Landeskunde 1882). Reck, Philipp George von, *An extract of the Journals of Mr. Com. von Reck and Rev. Mr. Bolzus,* (London 1734). Roll, Karl, *Die Schaumuenzen auf die Salzburger Emigration,* (Halle 1925). Scheitberger, Joseph, *Neu-vermehrter evangelischer Send-Brief, darinnen 24 nuetzliche Buechlein enthalten,* (Reutlingen). Schelhorn, Johann G., *Historische Nachricht vom Ursprunge, Fortgang und Schicksale der Evan. Religion in den Salzburgischen Landen,* (Leipzig 1732); (A series of pamphlets written by August F. Mueller, Samuel B. Walther, Siegmund Winkler, Johann G. Erlmann). Schwesinger M., (Editor) *Salzburger Emigration,* (Munich 1632). Swarzenski, Georg, *Die Salzburger Malerei, von den Ersten Anfaengen Bis Zur Bluetezeit Des Romantischen Stils,* (Leipzig 1913). Strobel, Philip A., *The Salzburgers and their Descendants,* (Athens, Georgia, 1953). Thompson, James Westphall, *The Middle Ages,* (New York 1931). Urlsperger, Samuel, *Ausfuehrliche Nachricht von den Salzburgischen Emigranten Die sich in Amerika niedergelassen haben,* (Halle 1744-). A day to day report on the Salzburgers from the day they were assembled at Augsburg, Germany, their travel to Rotterdam to England and to America and extending over a period of years while in Ebenezer. Volk, W., (Ludwig Clarus) *Die Auswanderung der protestantisch Gesinnten Salzburger in den Jahren* 1731 *u.* 1732, (Innsbruck 1864). *Vorstellungschreiben an Ihre Roemische Kaiserliche Majaestaet vom Corpus Evangelicorum,* (Regensburg Oct. 27, 1731). Wallace, Paul A., *The Muehlenbergs of Pennsylvania,* (U. of Pa. Press, 1949). Wegele, Ludwig, *Augsburg,* (Augsburg 1953). Widmann, Hans, *Geschichte Salzburgs* 3 Vols., (Gotha 1907). Zorn, Wolfgang, *Augsburg. Geschichte einer Stadt; (Augsburg),* and *Die Evangelische Kirche in Bayern,* (Munich). *Wolfgang Samuel u. Johann August Urlsperger, Zuverlaessige Relation, von Ankunft u. Aufnahme d. Salzburgischen Emigranten bei denen Evan. in Kaufbaeueren Augsburg, Memmingen, Ulm, Noerdlingen u. andern Schwaebischen Staedten,* (Munich).

DATE DUE

GAYLORD

PRINTED IN U.S.A.